How to Analyze People
& Dark Psychology

Identifying Covert Manipulation Tactics to Discover Intention and Take Back Control

HENRY WOOD

TABLE OF CONTENTS

HOW TO ANALYZE PEOPLE

TABLE OF CONTENTS
DARK PSYCHOLOGY

HOW TO ANALYZE PEOPLE

Who is Behind Them? The Complete Guide to
Discover Dark People's Masks through Analyzing
Body Language and Behavioral Psychology

HENRY WOOD

INTRODUCTION

Psychological analysis is a technique that requires years of learning, but thanks to several small foundations, you can get something close to accuracy.

The time required to pass knowledge is worthwhile. Many people are educated and equipped with intelligence and such knowledge is generally more accepted by them compared to those who are ignorant and do not have that "intelligent light."

Well, the reason these wise people are so good is often because they analyze the situation and people, shape themselves, and understand how these people think. This analysis is usually performed automatically by highly intelligent people but can be achieved or refined through research.

What you need to clarify when doing the analysis is that observation is fundamental, and everything is based on it. For every small nuance that a person plays, you need to be able to see all the little details.

Each reaction, movement, or way of thinking is caused by something, and this in turn causes other things as well. This means that if B triggers A, then we can also know C, D, and E because they are also triggered by B.

This allows you to know how people react to several things, how they can influence you and make you play in their favor.

All that is needed to analyze it is the right eye, which takes examples of others. This means that those who have never contacted people will notice that the details are not similar. You must rely on other previously known cases to determine the reason for each situation.

Psychological analysis cannot be summarized into a single entry, nor can it be done without practice or dedication.

CHAPTER 1

HOW TO ANALYZE PEOPLE WITH BEHAVIOURAL PSYCHOLOGY

Perceiving other people's feelings and thoughts is an important skill that helps you navigate interpersonal relationships. Every human being is different, but we are all wired the same way at the core level. Here, we start by recognizing subtle clues for a moment.

Establish baseline

I know people. To be able to read someone properly, you need to know them well. Knowing someone personally makes you more aware of their likes and dislikes, what their common habits are, and what is not necessarily "spoken." Take note of the following:

- Establish a baseline based on one person's opinion as well as some encounters with others.
- For example, you might have a friend who is generally very reserved or anti-social. If so, their fear may not be a sign of lies or tension. When you meet them on the street, common sense makes them nervous or anxious.
- Pay attention to the habits of others. Do they always maintain eye contact? Does their voice

15

change when they are nervous? How do they act when they are angry, provoked or excited? This will lead you to what you are looking for when trying to read them.

Ask open-ended questions. When you are reading someone, you are watching and listening. What you are not doing is grabbing the conversation at the corner and guiding it in your direction. So, ask your question and get out of there. Sit down, relax, and enjoy the show.

- Open-ended questions allow them to speak more so that they can talk longer.
- It is best to ask appropriate questions. Asking "How is your family?" may give you a very messy response that doesn't help you to evaluate better the information you are looking for. You may be able to collect more personal information by asking "What book are you currently reading?"

Look for baseline conflicts. Something must be happening to an ordinarily loving person when he doesn't seem physically present and doesn't want to get close to anyone except with a 10-foot stick. The same behavior Boo Radley shows does not necessarily mean the same thing. If you analyze how people behave in daily life, be aware of things that do not make sense.

- If something seems to be missing, you need to ask why, at least initially. They may be exhausted, had a fight with their significant other, got angered by their boss, or have a small personal problem they're stuck in. Do not assume that it reflects your relationship with that person before you know all the details.

Work with the cluster. Looking at a single clue is not a reason to jump to a conclusion. After all, someone may be leaning on you just because the chair is not comfortable.

- Try to get clues from their words, tone, body, and face. If you get one from each and have a lineup of all of them, it's safe to continue. But of course, a good way to check if you are right is to just ask directly.

Please know your weaknesses. As a mere human being, you can be mistaken. If you see something pretty, you will like it. If you are wearing a finely tailored Italian suit, others will probably trust you.

Humans generally think of dangerous people as those who are drunk, walking around the street, and carrying knives. In reality, most psychopaths are attractive and act properly in public. While it is virtually impossible to control, and although it is not necessarily the best or most accurate technique, the subconscious tells you to judge the book by its cover.

CHAPTER 2

THE BASICS OF HUMAN BEHAVIOR

The epistemology of the social sciences is engaged in a scientific debate, which gives rise to positions between explanation and understanding. Knowledge of the social is, therefore, first of all, a problem that results in opposition. These oppositions are inevitably embodied in the game of practices. It is, therefore, necessary to take time to reflect on these contradictory arguments in the midst of which the practitioner-researcher finds himself. Perhaps it would be possible to take a critical look at it with the premise that any explanatory claim accounts for reality only within its language. The explanation emphasizes the large units, the distance from the object, the structures. The explanation will tend to think of society by emphasizing the exteriority and the constraint specific to social facts. Understanding emphasizes the individuals in relation, the meanings, and the reflexivity of individuals and groups. Understanding will put more emphasis on understanding social action. These two epistemological postures respectively bring out other dualities: objectivity and subjectivity, proximity and distance; exteriority and interiority; structure, and meaning. However, in practice, these vectors become entangled despite the rational: structure and meaning.

The choice of words is very important when it comes to defining the individual. We must also choose those which account as clearly as possible for the study of the theories which seek to define it. The notion of social representation opens an interesting avenue to the idea of putting into action or, if you prefer, staging the relationship with the other through the approaches that stem from theories of human behavior. However, there is perhaps a lack of the "constructive" dimension of the individual and social relationships. We could grasp them as social constructs, which, in turn, are building elements of the individual and society.

Also, the different modes of apprehension of the individual are here conceived as being systems of logic, which give form to the individual. Whereas, conversely, the subject in the clinic, that is to say, in the exchange with the practitioner, gives birth to other avenues of research. You have to reckon with the creativity of individuals, which opens up large areas of existence. This inventiveness is found in the register of the intimate, the symbolic, of what remains hidden, in the shadows, and yet which creeps daily into the intervention. The term "construction" does not give enough account of the formal dimension (Simmel) of languages. In essence, these languages, in the image of form rather than structure, are effectively permeable to the movement of the social, even only in the clinic. We tend to abuse this notion of "construction" which shows rigid structures, reducible to systems of constraints and determination that must be "deconstructed." Configuration for the individual is formed and configured within the limits of each of the individual's (production) theories only. Suffice to say that each of the theories has a very relative knowledge of the individual and that the latter escapes the most complex theoretical scaffolding.

Conversely, these languages are necessarily transformed and reconfigured from clinical interaction. Here we abandon the belief in a finalized theoretical structure. For example, group and family psychoanalytic approaches appeared amid a strong current where, under the systemic influence, the interaction had become central to psychotherapeutic thinking. The individual was then less thought in isolation as it was traditionally represented in psychoanalytic treatment, than in interaction with his environment. Finally, this configuration of the individual is carried out from perspectives that come either from evidence favored by neo-positivism or from the symbolic universe or even from a project of social transformation. Although theories of human behavior cannot be reduced to one another, they are in continuous relation.

Furthermore, the study of theories of human behavior necessarily involves the study of the subject/object relationship. In this context, it may be useful here to reconsider the idea of flawless objectivity. It turns out that the practitioner-researcher and his object, unlike other fields, are of the same nature, which, it must be said, complicates things in explaining behavior. There are indeed different modes of apprehension, which leads us to think that everything is in the way of seeing. Now, is objectivity possible? Finding and selecting facts is not objective. The facts themselves are not objective, and even if it is hard information, the facts give rise to a set of beliefs from which the observer cannot escape.

The concept of objectivity is fragile. And yet, we must strive for certain objectivity. The role of the practitioner-researcher is not simply to assert his subjectivity, nor by pretending to be neutral, contenting himself with declaiming the grammar proper to his favorite theory. But still, recognizing one's subjectivity is not everything; it is necessary to distance oneself for the analysis. From the moment we conceive of the subject/object relationship as being unquestionably mediated by one or other of these representations or, to put it metaphorically in the manner of Wittgenstein (2003), by a particular mesh of the net theoretical, it is, therefore, the mesh of the net itself that must be taken care of. And since it is logically impossible to eliminate the subjectivity inherent in any observation of the human, it is, therefore, necessary to introduce this disturbing element, according to some, as an essential component of knowledge.

This is why the study of human behavior is, first of all, work on the observer, the one who projects his net forward on the object of his observation. This work on oneself as an observer is at the base of the ethics of the relation to the other. This work is not simply a psychological introspection through the current proposition, which sometimes reaches heights of convenience, "knowing yourself," although it involves the need for self-knowledge. This demanding work consists in questioning the "act of seeing" itself. The act of seeing is to be reinserted in the social context of its production. So, we interpret human behavior as we see it, that is to say within a particular theoretical language. This language must itself be placed in the context of its production. We see the sign "act missed" in the context of psychoanalysis. We see the sign "lack of attention" in the context of cognitivism, yet the sign remains the same, that is to say, forgetfulness.

"The idea is placed like glasses on our nose, and we only look through the idea," says Wittgenstein (Chauviré, 1990: 76). All the more reason to question this posture when it comes to the field of human behavior. We do not have the appropriate measurement instruments or concepts to explain this kind of effect definitively. So how is the individual question in these theories and in the approaches that flow from them?

After this little clarification on knowledge, we propose three aspects related to the study of the theories and approaches of the individual which derive from them. The first deals with three perspectives on theories of human behavior: 1- transformation; 2- sense; 3- structure; the second aspect looks at the issue of complementarity enshrined in pragmatic pluralism; finally, the third is linked to the construction of the clinical report.

Three perspectives

All theory is the translation of the immediate data of experience into a new language. This language has its own rules, its categories. It is, therefore, within its own rules that each theory qualifies the real. Thus, certain discourses relate to structures, others to meaning, others to transformations. We already see that these qualifications of the real have an impact on the configuration of the individual. These logics are organized around distinct intelligibility schemes that Jean-Michel Berthelot brilliantly noted in his excellent work, L'Inelligence du social (1990): dialectic, actancial scheme, hermeneutics, structural scheme, functionality, and causality. These intelligibility schemes can be grouped two by two and thus correspond to a qualification of reality. Thus:

a) The dialectical and actancial modes underlie a world in constant transformation.
b) The structural and hermeneutical modes refer to meaning.
c) The functional and causal modes correspond to the socio structural universe.

Transformation

Dialectics flow, among others, from the historical materialism of Marx, while the actancial scheme is at the heart of interactionist programs. We must emphasize the differential nature of the transformation generated by these two logics. The theory of conflicts inspired by Marxism, coming under the persuasion, sees the individual as an alienated being. The personal equation of the individual will be of little significance in the discourse because it must be replaced in the big sets that are social classes, age, and gender. We find ourselves here in a logic that aims at the structural transformation. This transformation is understood as a process of going beyond contradictions to higher levels. The structural and feminist approach defended by certain schools of social work is one application. Individual problems must be placed in the broader context of the society that determines the problems. Indeed, we oppose here the systemic theory, which claims that incest, for example, is the symptom of family dysfunction. Incest is explained here as the expression of male power over women and children.

According to the structural approach, it is precisely in the structures of domination that the problem must be replaced. Each problem will, therefore, be placed within the framework of large groups: gender, ethnicity, place of belonging, etc. The reference to the large units designates vast social systems to which the subject does not have direct access, but which have an impact on the other aspects of his individual and social existence. This is what can be called the "objective" place that the subject occupies within the social. The reference to large groups is indeed mattered for analysis since it locates the individual in a macro-sociological way. The identification of the various affiliations gives solid indications, but these explanations are all relative because any meaning given by the actor seems to be determined only by social position.

The consequence will be to refer to psychology all questions relating to the meaning and to retain only the general principle that lifestyles are the products of class divisions.

Theories also found in the register of transformation arise from the actuarial scheme. Many things can be said about action. Parsons (1955) thus developed a sociology of action, an application of which is found in his analysis of the doctor/patient relationship. The action, in this case, is linked to social roles and has more to do this time with the functional scheme. Rather than transformation, we aim here for balance through the adjustment of the individual to his roles. Action that falls under the actancial scheme is considered rather as an intentional action. We are talking less about structural transformations than about the intersection of the social circles that transform society. Here, social space is a field of reciprocal actions. The actancial schema brings together a set of actors, but each of the theories about the actancial schema leads to the individual. It has a margin of play that allows it to develop strategies, therefore, to play with codes.

Furthermore, individual actions are defined by anticipating what others think. The quest for self is played out under the gaze of others. The phenomena are, therefore, thought to result from the behavior of the actors involved. We can attach to this scheme theories as varied as symbolic interactionism, phenomenology, ethnomethodology, and the sociology of action of Touraine (1973). The action here supposes the aggregation of individual acts that transform the social.

Meaning

Hermeneutics is the oldest way of understanding reality. Psychoanalysis and phenomenology, for example, are based on this logic, which seeks to construct meaning. We are here in the field of representations and symbolic thought. Interpretation will be seen as a fundamental way of being in the world. Thus, there is no difference in nature between common sense and scientific knowledge since everything is interpretation. Rather, the explanation relates to the individual's sense of their own experience. However, here everything happens as if one could pretend to think outside social frameworks. But we must first understand these questions in the current context of (medical) appropriation of human behavior. A distinction is made between experimental methodology and a principle of otherness. Comprehensive approaches pursue a questioning as to the experimental methodology whose theoretical models will possess a priori and which contain in themselves the explanation of the phenomena to be observed by directing the clinician's gaze. The problem lies in the level of intentionality at the origin of such a practice. That is to say, in its claim to define the real as if the theoretical grid were itself a natural object, the only possibility of explanation.

The principle of otherness implies a dialogical relationship rather. Psychoanalysis has made transference and countertransference one of its major themes. This phenomenon will first be perceived as a hindrance then admitted not only as being irrepressible but well at the heart of the treatment. It is perhaps in this that psychoanalysis passes from a science of observation to that of interpretation because it will be from the relationship itself that the analyst will grasp a sense of the psychic discomfort of the other. For Eugène Enriquez (1993), the unconscious takes place at all levels of language. It arouses links and is, in turn, aroused by these links. Thus, the unconscious would be at work not only in the individual but in society as a whole.

Psychosociological approaches also claim to be hermeneutic. It is about worrying about the link established between the individual and society. We try to define problems according to the symbolic relationships of the individual with others. The individual seeks meaning in what is happening to him. In the school

27

environment, for example, it has been possible to establish a link between family problems and the child's difficulties. For example, it could be established that a child suffered from a school phobia due to his separation anxiety with a depressed mother. The psychosocial approach has a dynamic understanding of the problems experienced by the individual. The structural sphere here gives way to the socio-symbolic area because we are much more in the area of beliefs, subjectivity, and social representations. To become a social being, humans must learn to see themselves as outside about others, like others. The social observer is, therefore, dealing with a subjective world, whose behavior is endowed with meaning, symbolically constructed. There is the discourse on the other, but there is also the possibility of articulating a word and listening. This comprehensive posture allows the recognition of particular intelligibility. The observer who is interested in the object from its interiority must admit common sense, its subjectivity, and its imagination as constitutive of knowledge of the object. This model has been gradually evacuated by cognitive-behavioral approaches and whose lines are endowed with meaning, symbolically constructed.

Certain hermeneutic positions are also combined with the actuarial scheme. So, it is very common to meet hermeneutical and actancial schemes at the heart of the same programs. Individuals have a discursive consciousness that formulates rationalizations about actions. For Anthony Giddens (1987), who can be situated in the intersection of these two schemes, the actors can almost always formulate in a discursive way the intentions and the reasons for their actions. Discursive consciousness could correspond to Freudian consciousness. Actors, of course, do not have access to the unconscious motives for their actions, which is why the question of choice is almost always ambiguous. Giddens (1987) does not seem to us to insist enough on the existence of the unconscious. But, according to him, it is not necessary to worry unduly about what was not retained in the perception of the subject by seeking blockages and repressions. The unconscious calls upon modes of knowledge to which the subject does not have access. The intention is moreover not the sole fact of the individual but also of the interactions which he maintains with the surrounding culture. In other words, the daily interactions determine the intention in the same way as the psychology of the actor.

Individuals have a practical conscience. It refers to knowledge that the individual cannot express verbally, and its level depends on the routinization on which ontological security is based. Mechanisms, similar to the interaction rituals of Goffman (1974), protect ontological security. The predictability of routines is the cognitive mechanism that provides this security. However, "the radicalization of Modernity" has important consequences for this predictability because social life is now and unlike pre-modern societies, subject to continual change. The ever-greater distance between space and time, in a context of globalization, and the abstract relationships that this distancing generates effectively undermine confidence. Reflexivity, in this sense, is not just an individual conscience but a human way of building the social. Much remains to be done to uncover the mechanisms of reflexivity. However, when we talk about reflexivity, we are mostly talking about knowledge related to the meaning we give to our experience.

The second schema, which appeals to meaning, the structural model, produces intelligibility of behaviors whose meanings are not immediately obvious, and remain hidden at first sight from the eyes of the observer. In addition to Lévi-Strauss (1967), a famous representative of this vast program which establishes kinship structures through the play of oppositions and relationships between different terms, several observers of the family, particularly in psychotherapeutic circles, have highlighted the existence of myths at the foundation of families. They have also outlined the intergenerational transmission of certain symbols whose meaning is lost in the mists of time. Research shows that the intergenerational transmission of family secrets and myths is what constitutes the individual. From a structuralist perspective, it will be a question of understanding the regularities of cultures. It will be in the transgression of common codes that we will see pathologies appear. Family incest is a good example. These structures are cultural anchors which may differ from one culture to another, but which have certain universal traits. It is, therefore, possible to classify structures. In this context, the individual is inserted into these cultural anchors and therefore seems entirely determined by prohibitions and constraints. Contemporary modernity, however, sees certain structuring factors, most anchored in the collective unconscious, being transformed under the control of the individual.

Foucault (1988), who is interested in madness as an analyzer of social meanings, proceeds from this intellectual tradition, which seeks to formalize meaning. Instead of looking at the integrative values of society, he wonders what in society is excluded. The story of madness is indeed the story of the confinement of what was excluded. Throughout history, there is a universal ethnological status of madness.

The structural scheme, therefore, puts the terms of a structure of signs about association and opposition. A structure of meaning appears from the signs observed. Meaning takes on the attributes of meaning and is part of the collective rather than the individual.

Structure

The structures here are more akin to the idea of the system than of cultural structuring of which we spoke previously. The socio-structural universe puts in mechanical relation terms within a physical system that seeks to maintain its balance. The system needs demand that the element performs its function. Their social roles determine the individual. We are in the universe of constraint and exteriority. The functional variant is as follows: each element of the system has its function. This logic is at the heart of several theories in social sciences, the most famous clinical version of which is systemic.

Systems theory posits a certain number of principles: interaction, totality, organization, complexity, structural, and functional aspects of a system. We, therefore, pose here the interaction of systems as being primordial; systems communicate with each other, and clashes between them affect the individual. Social problems can be explained here by the community. The individual equation is of little significance in discourse. It is the whole that determines its parts. The family, for example, is seen as a whole that cannot be reduced to its elements. Individual behavior is described as a functional adaptation to the environment. Every system has an organizational structure. Thus, everything contributes to maintaining the balance of this structure. Actions are regulations of the system. This is why we talk about the functional aspect of a system. Understanding the interactions and finding meaning in the symptom will be considered useless for the system. One may wonder why it is so necessary for systemicians to deny the contribution of the unconscious; what is the place of the individual in the system, is he only an actor?

The systemic does not succeed in getting rid of certain machinery. Far from disappearing, this logic still largely dominates today, especially in ecosystem programs. According to this point of view, the behavior of the individual must be studied from the systems that make up his environment. There is a certain paradox in this discourse that has firmly turned to the side of living systems and asserts itself against experimentalism.

The ecosystem approach makes comparisons no longer with machines (software systems), but with other living systems. In this, it borrows too often from biological theses yet is clearly based on experimentalism. In the context of ecology, we also note the presence of causal logic. For example, a causal link will be established between a social factor and a behavior problem. We are relying here on the law of probabilities. A link will be established between factors of violence in childhood and the appearance of delinquency in adolescence. Note also that the ecological approach is very close to the behavioral approach.

Can we still speak of causal, the second scheme qualifying the social world from its structural exteriority? Certainly. No one will go so far as to claim clearly and without the slightest embarrassment today that a cause will always have the same effect. Rather, we speak of covariation between structural variables. However, the fundamental characteristic of this scheme will be to reduce the problems studied to models of mathematical relationships. Several programs that dominate these days widely are based on statistical methods. Think of the epidemiology, the social ecology, the behavioral theories that set the tone for most clinical interventions today.

Effective behavior is gradually acquired when rewarded for its consequences. This formulation by Thorndike (1898), cited in Ovide Fontaine's (1978: 51) work on behavioral therapies, constitutes the foundation of behavioral theory, later developed by Pavlov (1977) and Skinner (1971). If we stick to this proposition, we understand that the intervention will be oriented towards the idea of positive reinforcement of behaviors and of what we now call all "consequences." It will be noted here that the very words of the behavioral approach and the cognitive added value that it has gained in recent years have become common words in everyday speech. Conditioning, association, environment, learning, cognition are categories of construction of the individual relating to behavioral language.

Behavioral experimentation questions the free will of the human species and activates the debate between free choice and determinations. Behaviorism rejects the subjective method, accusing it of relying only on the subjective. It posits that phenomena should only be studied based on observable facts. Pavlov (1977) did make an important distinction between animals and humans, and that distinction was in the language he called "the second level of signaling." Behaviorist theories, however, have not entered the symbolism of language. It is a question here of reducing the explanation of a phenomenon to its cause, and this cause to its consequence. The studies are based on a nosography which currently dominates mainly in psychiatry.

The behavior modification approach is based on evidence: behavior. It has one objective: to modify undesirable behaviors. It will be noted here that the notion of undesirable is poorly defined as if there were objective reasons for explaining desirable or undesirable behavior. In any case, it refers to social norms and the duty-being, which is in agreement with these norms. It is, therefore, necessary to resort to behavior control. For example, Watson, in the 1950s, advised mothers to prevent homosexuality for boys. This reminds us that theories are linked to the social context of their production.

CHAPTER 3

COMMON PATTERNS OF HUMAN BEHAVIOUR

When certain reactions of the person become frequent in certain environments or situations, they constitute what we call a behavior pattern.

A behavior pattern is a constant way of thinking, feeling, reacting physically, and acting in a certain situation. Our behavior patterns stem from what we copy or learn from people who have shared life with us, such as our parents, grandparents, uncles, teachers, and any important person with whom we have had significant contact. They also come from our reactions, and this means that we keep within ourselves the reactions we have towards others. We record and save our reactions when we satisfy or don't satisfy needs and desires. Even our various reactions to hunger, thirst, contact, company, affection, security, protection, etc.

Everything is saved from being used at any other time. This means that everything we see and hear is captured in our way and stored in us, to be used as a "pattern of behavior," for better or for worse. All the reactions (ideas, thoughts, images, emotions, feelings, and physical sensations) that happen or are experienced are kept in records or "files" in each human being. These "recordings" will be exposed to ourselves and others. A behavior pattern can be constructive or destructive, and it has four components:

(1) Thoughts, beliefs, and ideas.

(2) Emotions, feelings, moods, and images.

(3) Behaviors, and finally

(4) Body reactions; which, when the pattern is destructive, generate tension, little energy, tremors, stress; it affects others and breaks relationships, etc.

When the patterns are constructive and involve behaviors appropriate to the situation, we experience feelings of peace and security, a firm attitude, clear words, and with an appropriate tone of voice and volume. Affirmations and judgments are based on proven facts, and things are appreciated as they are. As much as someone resembles another, they will never be the same because absolutely everyone has a very particular way of being and facing the facts of life. Each person has certain characteristics and patterns of behavior that help or hinder development. Each person has certain characteristics, but there are specific behavior patterns that distinguish them from the rest. For balanced human development, it will be necessary to recognize what my behavior patterns are, and if they are constructive or, on the contrary, if they are destructive for me and others.

CHAPTER 4

UNDERSTANDING & ANALYZING PERSONALITY TYPES

The study of personality should be done, taking into account that the person develops in situations, which in turn are immersed in a certain society or culture—the importance of studying the situation.

It is already well known in personality research that the weight of personal variables in the explanation of behavior will depend on the degree of the structuring of situations: if situations are highly structured, the possibilities of individual variation are almost nil; but as the situation becomes more ambiguous, differential behavioral manifestations appear among the individuals who confront it.

External determinant: Situation

Research data allows us to conclude that the interaction process must be studied as a unit of analysis, but without forgetting that the personal and situational variables integrated into the said process must be known. Although personal variables have been studied considerably, this does not happen with situational variables.

Magnusson points out three reasons that justify the analysis of the situation:

- Behavior takes place in situations; it only exists in the situation and cannot be understood without it.
- Consideration of the situation in theories will contribute to more functional models of behavior explanation.
- A more systematic understanding of situations will contribute to more effective explanations in psychology. In any case, the study of situations in personality is not a goal in itself but is motivated by the need for a more effective theory, research, and application of knowledge about the personality of individuals.

Analysis of The Situation

The external world can be organized according to two levels of amplitude; macro, and micro, depending on its proximity to the individual. In turn, there will be physical or objective characteristics and social, psychological, or subjective characteristics:

- **The macro-physical environment:** the streets, parks, buildings, etc.
- **The micro-physical environment:** the furniture and objects in the room.

- **The macro-social environment:** the laws, norms, or values that are common to a society or culture.
- **The micro-social environment:** the norms, attitudes, habits, etc. of the groups and people with whom an individual interacts directly. It is, at least to some degree, unique to each individual or group.

Another way to characterize the analysis of the external world is in terms of the duration of its influence. Endler defines the environment as the most general and persistent context in which the behavior occurs, while the situation would be the momentary and passing framework. The stimuli would be the elements within the situation.

Approaches to the study of the situation in psychology: The situation can be analyzed from three different perspectives:

Ecological or environmental perspective: Analyzes the environments in terms of the physical characteristics under which the behavior takes place. This is based on the assumption that they exert more influence on the behavior than the person's characteristics. That is, they focus on the objective environment, regardless of the psychological processes that people feel in it. The basic unit of study is the behavioral scenarios (environments that occur naturally, not having been created by the experimenter) with the following properties:

They include fixed patterns of behavior foreign to individuals within specific spatio-temporal coordinates.

They consider sets of elements of the scenario to be non-behavioral (physical).

It is understood that there is an interdependence between the physical, temporal, and geographical characteristics of the environment and the proper patterns of behavior.

Thus, the behavior scenario has physical limits. The psychological environment is a subjective representation of the objective situation that the person makes at a given moment. The ecological environment has a more lasting and objective existence, independent of the psychological processes of a specific person.

The study of behavioral scenarios allows studying community programs, churches, school classes, etc. They are situations so structured that the weight of personal variables in predicting behavior is minimal.

Behavioral perspective: Environments are described in terms of their structure (physical characteristics) and their stimulating function (reinforces, punishes, etc.). People can actively participate in their relationship with

41

the environment, but that does not mean that they are autonomous agents in the control of their behaviors.

Social perspectives: They study social episodes (sequences of interaction that constitute natural units of behavior and that are distinguished because they have symbolic, temporal and physical limits). Attention is paid to the cognitive perception and representation of situations. These three perspectives differ in 3 aspects:

- The emphasis is given to personal characteristics.
- The weight is given to the objective vs. subjective aspects of the situation.
- Your consideration of space and time.

Approaches to the study of the situation in personality psychology: From which the subjective or perceived nature of the situation has been emphasized, and that the study of the situation is not an objective in itself, but a necessity to make better predictions of behavior. Situation taxonomies must meet three requirements:

- **Domain:** They reflect situations in which the researcher samples at his convenience (for example, stressful, work, academic).
- **Units of analysis:** They must specify them to classify the situations.
- **Consideration of the situation:** Specify whether they are aimed at classifying objective or psychological situations.

The approach based on the perception of the situation: Situations can be analyzed based on how they are perceived and interpreted, that is, based on their stimulating value. In general, two main strategies have been used:

- **Judgments of inter-situational similarity:** In which subjects are asked to judge the similarity between the situations presented through verbal descriptions, analyzing the data with FA. The results show a high agreement between the perceivers on the similarity between situations.

- **Prototype analysis:** Prototypes or ideal examples of a category are used. It is assumed that situations have a variety of attributes that are perceived and interpreted by individuals, according to cognitive schematics of situations that the individual has from previous experiences. Thus, an individual who faces a situation compares the attributes of the situation with those of the cognitive prototype that he already possesses. This strategy allows: To establish taxonomy of the commonly used categories of situations (for example, social, cultural, political, etc.) which, in turn, are hierarchically ordered (from the most inclusive or superordinate to the most subordinate).

If we ask the subjects to generate prototypes, the agreed prototype can be obtained (averaging the characteristics listed by the subjects). These prototypes suggest that people share sets of beliefs about the characteristics of various situations, or the behaviors expected of them. We can use consensus prototypes to test hypotheses.

Cantor measured similarity between prototypes, finding that those belonging to the same category had more elements in common than those from different categories. It seems, then, that an important part of the common knowledge of situations would be psychological (prototypes provide the individual with expectations about the most probable or socially appropriate behaviors in situations).

He also measured the time it took for subjects to form the image after reading the stimulus, and found that situations are imagined faster, and then people in situations, and finally, people. So, it seems that there are differences in terms of accessibility and richness of this information.

Also, he studied the attributes of situations. The results show that the frequency of the events that describe the physical nature of the situation, and the people present in it, are greater in the prototypes of specific or subordinate categories; while in the more abstract, aspects of a psychological nature prevail.

From this approach, it is possible to analyze which behaviors the subjects anticipate as most probable in a specific situation. The more prototypical a situation is, the more consensuses there is about the behaviors that will be carried out in it.

The approach based on the reaction to the situation:

Rotter proposed classifying situations based on the similarity of behavior they generate in people, suggesting using the following procedures:

- Resort to expert judgment.
- Take the judgment of subjects from the same culture or group as the one being evaluated.
- Analyze the frequency of specific kinds of behavior in certain situations.
- Measure the expectation that certain reinforcements or consequences will occur in those situations.
- Determine the nature (academic, work, affective, etc.) and the sign of reinforcement (positive or negative) that is most likely to occur in the situation.
- Study the gradients of generalization of changes that occur in behavior, expectations, or values of reinforcement. The generalization gradient indicates similarity.

In addition to these procedures, others have been used:

ER inventories: present the verbal description of situations related to some variable that we want to measure (anxiety, pleasure), asking the subject to report the degree to which they experience somatic or psychic reactions. A famous example is Wolpe's Systematic Desensitization technique, where patients develop a hierarchy of subjective anxieties.

In the person-situation pairing technique, the situation is characterized as a pattern of behavior for an ideal type of person. The behavior of a person in a situation will depend on the similarity between the characteristics of the person and the ideal pattern of behavior of the individual-type corresponding to that situation.

Bem proposes that a person be analyzed in terms of how they respond to a set of hypothetical situations. The similarity between two situations would depend on the number of main elements they share, the number of unique elements of one or the other, and the degree to which their characteristics (shared and non-shared) are distinctive within the set of compared situations.

Pervin asks each subject to:

- Make a list of real-life situations (each person's place, people, time, and activities).
- Describe each situation, to generate a list of attributes.
- Describe your feelings in them, to make a list of feelings for each situation.
- Describe your behavior, generating a list of behaviors.

- Judge, once the lists are made, the degree to which each aspect of the three lists applies to each situation.

In this way, he obtains information about the individual's real situations and their characteristics. Another taxonomy based on people's consensus on the conceptualization of situations is that of Van, who built lists of attributes for each situation, interviewing 160 subjects.

Six hundred and fifty-nine attributes belonging to the categories resulted: context, physical environment or location, objective characteristics of the physical environment, people, objective characteristics of people, activities, equipment or objects, and temporal aspects. Thus, ten situational factors (intimacy, leisure, conflict, etc.) that can be used to predict the behavior that can occur in the different categories were identified.

The approach based on situational preferences:

Analyze what kinds of situations are chosen by the subjects. People avoid certain situations and choose others; they can modify situations to suit their characteristics, and they can create situations that facilitate certain behaviors. Personal characteristics influence the choice of one or the other.

Other aspects, such as environmental and cultural pressures, or the real possibility of accessing them, also intervene in these elections.

The approach based on personality traits:

One way to construct a taxonomy of personality traits that systematically captures situational information, would be by asking a high number of subjects, for each characteristic of the Five Factors, to indicate situations or behaviors that are typically associated with that trait. In this way, we would know the situations that best allow the expression of a certain trait.

Ten Berge and De Raad

They constructed a repertoire, based on descriptions of subjects, about the situations in which a certain personality characteristic was shown. They obtained 237 situations that they classified according to how much each participant could deal with it. The idea was that the ways of relating to situations imply coping styles (dispositional or personal tendencies). From this perspective, certain types of people may have preferences for situations that are different from those shown by other people; certain situations would allow more behavioral variation, and people characterized by a certain trait may have a greater preference for those situations that allow the expression of that trait. The results show a 4-factor structure:

- Pleasure situations
- Adverse situations for the individual
- Situations of interpersonal conflict
- Situations of social demand

Generally speaking, people who score high on one of the five factors are better at dealing with situations associated with that factor. There are many situations in which extraverted, emotionally stable, and open to experience people are better off than introverted, unstable, and closed to experience.

However, affability and tenacity are more specific factors of the situation (they are character factors, while Extraversion, emotional stability, and openness are of temperament).

Culture

Personality does not refer to connotations of dignity or prestige; that is, it is free of values. However, the psychology of personality is driven by certain social and cultural values that can affect our interpretations of behavior. These cultural aspects are important because, possibly, they determine many psychological processes and affect the personality (the very concept of oneself or self).

Concept and implications. Culture includes what is transmitted from generation to generation in a given society: procedures, habits, norms, beliefs, and shared values that also affect information that is considered important. Individuals differ in the extent to which they adopt and fulfill the values and behaviors of the cultural group to which they belong, and it is even possible to speak of different subcultures within the same culture.

The process by which a culture is transmitted is acculturation. As a result of this process, we can interact with people from our own culture because we share the same verbal and non-verbal language.

Cultures differ in fundamental aspects such as:

- Man's view of human nature as essentially good, positive, bad, or perverse, as well as the degree to which the possibility of personal change is defended.
- Man's relationship with nature. In industrialized societies, nature is at the service of man; in indigenous populations, man depends on nature; in eastern societies, tranquility is achieved by being in harmony with nature.
- The way of understanding time. In the west, the future prevails, in southern Europe, the present, and the east of England, the past and tradition.

The Most Valued Personality Type.

The usual forms of relationship between members. In individualistic societies, it is expected to obtain personal satisfaction from the relationship with others. In collectivists, harmony in relationships and the collaboration of each person to collective well-being are valued.

Furthermore, cultures are influenced by ecological variables. For example, high reliefs reduce the probability of cultural diffusion, making the culture homogeneous.

Cultural dimensions

Cultures differ in complexity, the indices of which are: per capita income, size of cities, percentage of urban versus rural population, computers per person, etc. In complexes, there are more possibilities of choice and lifestyles.

They also differ in the rigidity of their standards. Isolated societies tend to be airtight (neighboring societies do not influence them), have clear ideas about appropriate behavior, and apply sanctions to people who do not follow the rules. In relaxed cultures, the deviation is tolerated.

Cultures also differ in their individualistic or collectivist character. The more complex a culture is, the more likely it is to be individualistic; the more rigid its norms, the more likely it is that it is collectivist. In individualistic societies, people are autonomous and independent from their groups, prioritize their goals, and emphasize autonomy, the right to privacy, etc.

In the collectivists, the collective identity, dependency, group solidarity, sharing duties, and group decision are emphasized. To define culture as individualistic or collectivist, the following is taken into account:

- How the self is defined, which can emphasize personal or collective aspects.
- Which goals have higher priority, personal or group?
- What kinds of relationships are enhanced between its members, those of exchange or equality?
- What are the most important determinants of social behavior, whether they are attitudes or norms?

Within collectivism and individualism, there are many varieties. The most analyzed dimension is the horizontality-verticality of relationships, depending on whether equality or hierarchy is emphasized, respectively. There are four types of cultures:

- **Individualistic-horizontal:** independence prevails. People want to be unique and different from groups.
- **Individualistic-vertical:** people want to differentiate themselves and also be the best. There is high competitiveness.

- **Collective-horizontal:** people cooperate with their group, common goals are emphasized, but they do not submit to authority easily.
- **Collective-vertical:** people submit to the authority of the group and can sacrifice themselves for the interest of the group. They are traditionalist cultures.

When we refer to the personality of these cultures, we speak of 60% allocentric in collectivist cultures and 60% idiocentric in individualistic. The allocentric emphasize the interdependence, sociability, and family integrity, and take into account the needs and desires of the members of their group. The idiocentric ones emphasize self-exaltation, competitiveness, the unique character of the person, hedonism, and the emotional distance of the group.

CHAPTER 5

WHAT'S DARK PSYCHOLOGY?

The behaviors that are included within the triad of dark psychology are called narcissism, psychopathy, and Machiavellianism. These behaviors are generally what a "bad person" has.

But what is each one about? Narcissism is present in people who are self-centered, and everything they do, think and say, always has to do with personal gain. This type of personality does not think about the well-being of others, but only about his own. These people generally need the admiration of others and believe that their power is unlimited.

Psychopathy is a lack of empathy. This way of being is accompanied by the first, generating that the person is manipulative, and always achieves what he wants without thinking of others. Another characteristic is the lack of honesty, and they are disinterested in the feelings of other people, including those closest to them.

The last of these behaviors is Machiavellianism. It is present in people who always seek to benefit their interests and have cynical attitudes.

Although these are known as the "dark triad" of psychology, studies indicate that a fourth behavior should be added: sadism, understood as satisfaction with the suffering of others. Sadistic people enjoy psychological pain with other people.

Behaviors listed by Dark Psychology

This is the list of behaviors that people who make up the "dark triad" have:

- Handling
- Always want to be in control of situations
- Pressuring others to achieve what you want
- Harm to another person
- Teasing someone to make them angry
- Hurting other people, including those with whom you have empathy

Psychologists and professionals have thoroughly studied these ways of acting and have written numerous essays. They indicate that there are people who exhibit any of the behaviors listed above, but that this does not mean that these individuals are "bad people." The inconvenience arises when these ways of thinking and acting begin to interfere with daily life and become a problem that needs to be solved.

CHAPTER 6

THE 4 DARK PSYCHOLOGY TRAITS

Many that are not capable of communicating with others or who are capable of actively disconnecting from their feelings are usually part of the dark triad. It is a set of personality characteristics that define narcissism, Sadism, Machiavellianism, and psychopathy.

At the most extreme level, individuals who share the traits of this triad become true criminals or get lost in the broad spectrum of mental illness. But some do not meet the criteria for a psychiatric diagnosis and live with us daily.

Thus, those who exhibit these traits and forms of behavior possess what is called obscure personalities because of their insensitive, selfish, and malicious tendencies in their relationships with others. Delroy Paulhus and Kevin-Williams, psychologists at the University of British Columbia, are those who have dubbed the most negative part of human relationships as the black triad. Let's see what this triad consists of.

Narcissism

"I have the right to do anything" or "Others exist only to worship me" are examples of thoughts dominated by narcissism. These are selfish people, with an egocentric sense of the law and a positive self-image, although not very realistic if we take into account the vision of those around them.

Narcissists are "snake charmers." At first, they are highly appreciated by others—their behavior is pleasant and admirable—but, as time goes by, they can become very dangerous. They may even unintentionally let others see what their true intentions are: to receive more admiration and power.

They are often bored with routine and seek difficult challenges. That's why most narcissists are committed to politics, the law, or some other occupation that requires high-stress rates. Narcissism is, according to psychoanalyst, Michael Maccoby, an increasingly common condition in the upper hierarchy of the entrepreneurial sector, and is directly linked to competitiveness, income, and glamour.

One of their strengths is the great capacity for the conviction that they possess. Thanks to her, they surround themselves with a large number of followers and can convince them of what they want without making the slightest effort; ultimately succeeding in doing whatever they set out to do. Furthermore, since they lack empathy, this does not cause them any difficulty; they are not conscientious at all with the means and strategies they can use to achieve their goals.

The interest and concern of narcissistic people for others is zero, despite their great theatricality. They feel no remorse and are impassive when faced with the needs and feelings of the people around them.

Their Achilles heel is their self-esteem. Narcissists generally have very poor self-esteem, which goes hand in hand with internal vulnerability and some instability. Thus, they frequently try to bond with people whom they consider inferior to exercise their domination and to feel powerful.

Machiavellianism

For the "Machiavellians," the end justifies the means, whatever the consequences that may arise. They are usually very cold and calculating people who destroy any real emotional connection with others. Even if they normally have traits in common with narcissists, such as their selfishness and the use of others, one point differentiates them. In essence, they are realistic in the perceptions and estimates that they have of their skills, in addition to the relationships that they maintain.

The "Machiavellians" do not try to impress others, on the contrary. They present themselves as they are and choose to see things as they can handle them better in this way. In reality, they are relying on the emotions of the people they want to exploit to do what they want better. When they predict their emotions, they'll find it easier to put a plan in motion.

According to Daniel Goleman, psychologist, people with Machiavellian characteristics have poorer empathic tuning with others. Their coldness tends to stem from a deficit in emotion control, either their own or others'.

Emotions are so disconcerting to Machiavellian people that when they feel anxious, they don't know if they are feeling sad, tired, or just plain sick. However, they have a great ability to sense what other people think. But as Goleman says, "Even if their heads know what to do, their hearts continue to have no idea."

Sadism

Sadism is a feeling attributable to a living being, which consists of feeling pleasure, causing another animated being physical or mental damage that causes pain. The active subject of sadism can be an animal, like the cat that plays with its prey and seems to enjoy its actions, although we do not know if it does this consciously or not. That is why sadism is generally applied to voluntary (malicious) human actions such as the case of someone who tortures an animal or a person enjoying their cruelty. Examples: "Juan is a sadistic boy; he enjoys hitting his pets" or "The kidnapper expressed his sadism by chaining his victim with barbed wires."

Sadism is a term that comes from the deviant sexual behavior of the French writer known as Marquis de Sade (1740-1814). He was famous for his scandals and orgies that he starred in addition to writing novels that reflected libertine violence. However, sadism includes not only these practices of paraphilia (that is, acts of domination, humiliation, or physical and moral violence, with sexual connotations) but also everything that hurts another for the enjoyment of the sadist. In sexual sadism, death drives are combined with sexual drives. It appears according to Freud in his psychoanalytic theory, as a drive in the development phase called oral sadist (which is linked to biting and appears between six months and two years) and anal sadist (between two and four years of age, where the child feels pleasure when he controls his intestines). For Lacan, it is a form of perversion, like masochism, exhibitionism, and voyeurism.

If we unite a sexual sadist with a masochist (who likes to suffer), we obtain the figure of sadomasochism, wherewith we see complicity of victim and victimizer. The first receives mistreatment and enjoys it in a sexual act, like the sadist in a necessary and agreed pair.

Psychopathy, The Most Dangerous Personality of The Black Triad

Psychopaths see others as objects they can use and throw away as they please. However, unlike other personalities in the black triad, they rarely feel anxious and even seem to ignore what it means to be afraid.

The coldness of the psychopath is extreme; he can, therefore, become much more dangerous than the rest of the personalities of the black triad.

Thus, by not feeling this fear, they can remain calm even in emotionally intense, dangerous, and terrifying situations. The consequences of their actions are not at all important to them. They are the best candidates to end up in prison.

The neural circuits of this type of personality numb the emotional spectrum associated with suffering. Their cruelty resembles insensitivity because they are unable to detect it. Furthermore, remorse and shame do not exist for them either.

Finally, psychopaths have a certain facility for putting themselves in the shoes of others and pressing the appropriate buttons to achieve their objective. They have a great capacity for persuasion. Despite everything, this type of people, even if they stand out in terms of social cognition, are characterized by their understanding of the relationships and behavior of others from a logical or intellectual point of view.

As we see, it seems that the dark side implemented by the Sith in Star Wars is not as unreal as we might think. The presence of this black triad in intimate relationships leads to ill-treatment through psychological violence. These are poisonous figures who establish circles of power, control, and hostility and mentally trap their victims.

The trick to not falling into their traps is focusing on our freedom from emotions. To know how to set clear limits in our relationships and not allow someone to exceed them. Protecting ourselves must be our priority in all types of relationships.

CHAPTER 7

DO WE ALL HAVE A DARK SIDE?

Discovering your dark side is not an easy task, mainly because the "dark side" is that part of us that, many times, we still have not accepted.

Have you ever wondered why you can't stand that certain person?

In this chapter, I hope I can answer this question and offer you some clues to discover that part of you that you may not like so much, but that also needs to be recognized, accepted, and integrated.

The shadow

As a child, you receive a significant amount of judgments about what is right and what is wrong about you, your behavior, or your feelings. So at a very young age, you already have a clear idea of what is appreciated and valued by your parents, and what is not.

For example, if your parents criticize you for crying, you learn that showing strength is recognized and accepted, but showing weakness is not. Every time you feel weak, you will give up that feeling and send it to the subconscious or shadow.

63

Thus, it will be created as a "bag" in which each behavior that is criticized, each thought that is despised or each emotion that is not valued, will be sent to the subconscious. You will abandon any relationship with the rejected part.

That subconscious could also be represented by the part of the iceberg that you don't see.

But, to put it in some way, you cannot stay in the subconscious either because whatever you have rejected is part of you, so your subconscious will send your rejected part to your conscience, but backward.

How about the reverse?

Why does the other's behavior bother you?

Let's continue with the previous example. If weakness is rejected as an emotion, by adults or by society, you will also reject it, and you will not want to know anything about it.

So, two things can happen:

1. You will not be able to recognize weakness in yourself, but you will be able to see it in others, and you will not bear it.
2. You may be able to recognize weakness in yourself, but you cannot afford it so that you will deny and reject it.

And this is how you learn to project onto others those rejected parts of yourself.

Can't stand the pushy people?

What if I tell you that one of these two things may be happening to you?

That you have your share of arrogance, but that you are unable to see it or, that you see it, but you do not allow it, because there is a negative judgment in your mind that prevents it.

Really, how bad is arrogance or weakness?

It will depend on the situation, the moment, the person in front of you...

- Do you need to show strength always?
- Can you afford weakness in certain situations?
- Can you be pushy with people or situations when necessary?

Because that is the crux of the matter and, the most important thing: to be able to show you in each situation, from your authenticity and sometimes, also, as the situation requires.

The two ways to discover your dark side

I've already explained the two ways to you with an example to make it easier to understand, but let's now try to discover more parts of your shadow.

65

Find those characteristics, behaviors, or feelings of other people that bother you.

It is important to not the latter part, "that bother you," because if you do not like these behaviors, but they do not move anything inside you, they may not have anything to do with you.

You have to look for those behaviors, emotions, or people that you do not support, that make your blood run down when you see them. Not those that leave you indifferent... and there, you will have a clue of something that perhaps you may be rejecting.

Once these behaviors, feelings, or qualities of these people have been located, try to look inside yourself and ask yourself the following questions.

That which bothers you, have you ever experienced it in yourself?

And, if so, have you allowed yourself? Have you been able to express it?

Imagine that you have felt it, but you have not allowed it.

Now that you've seen it, could you stand it?

Could you afford to be a little weak or a little pushy?

Could you try to do it today?

Could you accept that part of you?

Integrate your shadow

When you do this exercise, you will be able to see what you have been rejecting, and it will be time to recognize it in order to integrate it into your consciousness.

As you already know, life is a combination of opposites: there is no night without day, darkness without light, inhalation without exhalation...

So, once you have your list made, it will be time to accept those parts you have discovered:

1. Re-appropriating the projection: recognize that others are a mirror where you can look at yourself and see both your most positive and negative aspects.

And although this section tries to discover your dark side, you can also do the exercise to discover your most positive side, trying to make a list of people you admire the most.

Write down those behaviors, feelings, or actions that you value from these people and look for them inside you.

I am sure you will find them because one can only see what is in you. And if it resonates in you, then you also possess that quality. If it was not so, you could not see it.

It is important that you also try to find that positive aspect in yourself, to integrate it as a part of yourself.

2. If you can recognize it, but cannot stand it, the time has come to practice

If you didn't allow yourself to be weak, give yourself small safe spaces where you can free yourself from the burden of having to "always" be strong.

Don't be afraid, because the more weakness you allow yourself, the more your strength grows.

This is how opposites work, the more you go to one side, the more ability you have to go to the other. Remember that weakness and strength are two sides of the same coin.

I assure you that once you integrate those parts into you, you will feel liberated because you no longer have to fight to avoid having certain feelings and, you use them when the need arises.

CHAPTER 8

WHAT IS THE DARK SIDE OF JOKER?

Joker is a clear example of the deterioration of a character before a society that defines seeing the inhuman side of a citizen as common and ordinary, as everyone else. All the illusions and intentions of standing out in life take away from him and in turn, psychologically, society makes him another victim of themselves.

Society embarrasses us all the time and has us on the brink of an absence of values, between which there is no difference between living with values or without values and how mediocrity defines the course of many people today. The most tragic thing is that although it is a movie, unfortunately, it highlights a real problem that we can see in all parts of the world.

Joaquín Phoenix will surprise you with a performance so spectacular that it will leave you speechless. And it is very rare to see today a character that shows true pain caused by a series of actions that mark tears, sadness, helplessness, and courage.

It would be truly unfair to make the comparison of this same character already played by other great people like Jack Nicholson, Heath Ledger, or Jared Leto.

Although Phoenix is one of the greats, this story will mark you and leave you with a bad taste in your mouth for the times we are living in.

Unfortunately, many of the stories we see on the screen today are recycled by Hollywood itself, which are changed and that use computerized effects or excessive use of techniques such as the famous green screen.

Tod Phillips is the director and is responsible for bringing this project to a level difficult for superhero lovers or villains to overcome. I dare say that this performance will be one of the most difficult to forget and that today it is already in the process of being one of the favorites, enough to give an Oscar to Joaquín Phoenix.

Now comes the moment of confusion. Do you think Batman is the villain after watching this movie? And the saddest thing, do you think we are far from this fiction?

Several media platforms have already announced a warning and controversy about the possible message it may leave on young people or weak minds.

Psychologists call this film a danger, and the expectation before the projection of this film keeps its eyes open to all the movie theaters that will exhibit JOKER.

CHAPTER 9

HOW TO DISCOVER DARK PEOPLE'S MASKS

Most people are happy, successful, or have a perfect life. Is that it? Hell, no. Most of them do not appear to be everything they are. That is what is called wearing a mask.

Depressed people who are optimistic, people with anxiety who are relaxed, people who wear a mask so that others do not see them as they are—these are all mask wearers. Do you want to know what are the masks we wear and their causes? Go ahead then!

The controller

A person who is controlling in every way of his life may be someone who has been previously betrayed. Faced with this pain, the person will develop a behavior that will allow him to ensure that others keep their promises. In this way, he will prevent them from betraying him again.

The controller has a hidden face, which is the known insecurity. For this reason, controlling everything is essential, sometimes even exaggerated. The mask protects you from the pain of a new betrayal while trying to keep it from happening again.

The rigid

A rigid person may have experienced a serious situation of injustice before this. He is inflexible in the face of this reality and still wants truth and the consistency of events.

A stiff person is a perfectionist. So much so that the mindset is obsessed. Yet, let's try to put ourselves in his place! We don't like injustices, and they get us confused. It is stipulated that having anything properly learned would prevent inequality from coming through the gates. That's why act so rigid.

The clerk

A dependent person may carry deep pain inside because of the feeling of abandonment. This wound causes detachment towards anyone so as not to feel abandoned again. This prevents them from taking any relationship seriously and they reject the idea of living with someone.

The pain of abandonment is terrible. The dependent person is not! On the contrary, he suffers in his innermost heart for not being able, if not depending on someone, to trust that those who are people important to him will never abandon him.

He who flees

The fleeing person refuses to be in the company of others. He prefers solitude, moments of calm. He refuses to be the center of attention, something that terrifies him. A person who runs away does so because he has been rejected, and that has caused him such an injury that he cannot avoid it.

Many who flee cannot bear not knowing how to behave, feel guilt, or feel helpless in certain circumstances because it's going to cause some to push them away. In their solitude, they are neither vulnerable nor insecure. This mask protects them from what hurts them. Is it cowardice? No. It is only to avoid what we know we cannot control or prevent from hurting us.

The masochist

Masochists can be mental or emotional. This attitude is given by a feeling of humiliation and shame as a result of a past situation. This causes his attitude always to be that of solving the problems of others, doing everything for them while lowering himself, and humiliating himself.

The masochist does not behave like the previous ones that avoid or try to escape their wounds. The masochist faces what hurts him in search of more pain. They hurt him, and he was not in control. Now he has it, and it is he who decides to harm himself. In his heart, this helps him deal with this situation.

As we have seen, there are several different and diverse masks that we can put on because of an emotional wound that we have suffered. Do you have any of the previous masks? Do you know someone who wears one? People wearing masks are easy to identify because, at some point, their hidden self appears.

It is best to overcome what has caused us fear. Perhaps the masochist is hard on himself, but at least he faces his pain. This can make him stronger, and he can overcome his trauma or, on the contrary, continue hurting himself. What do you think about all this?

CHAPTER 10

5 CLUES TO REVEAL TRUE INTENTIONS

When you find out that someone has hidden intentions, you may feel anxious about dealing with that person. In this chapter, we are going to look at five ways to spot hidden intentions and what you can do to prevent yourself from being manipulated.

There are undoubtedly very toxic people in the world, and chances are you have already met many. A person with hidden motives is likely to be selfish or narcissistic.

You will generally notice that many may seem sympathetic at first, but in the end, it is only a trick in order to get something from you later.

These individuals have bad intentions. They don't want to be your friend just for the sake of being your friend. On the contrary, they use patterns to manipulate you into doing things they want you to do.

So how do you identify these bad intentions in toxic people from the start? Some people are extremely subtle with their intent and may turn out to be the most amazing liars you could meet. But if you are able to notice any of these signs in a person, then you have probably spotted them before they can even take action.

Here are some clues to identify hidden intentions that someone has toward you and what you can do to avoid dealing with people who are trying to make you weak.

1. One idea in mind

They continue on their way with an obsession, which ends up bringing you to their submission. The only reason they do this to everyone is so that they can achieve whatever goal they have planned in this interaction. You may notice that they are constantly talking about the same things, in an attempt to make you get an idea into your head, so you can help them achieve what they're looking for.

Don't feel like you have to do anything. Refuse to give them what they want, even at the risk of repeating yourself. You can always say no, move on or completely withdraw from this situation.

2. Do you have a bad feeling?

You will feel misunderstood, irritated, uncertain, or you will simply have a very bad feeling after speaking with a toxic person; these signs generally indicate that you are the prey of a malicious person.

These people give you the feeling of not being heard, a bit like you are talking to a wall all the time. Don't be a victim of these negative feelings, because that's what they're looking for in the background. They feed on this energy and use it to their advantage.

3. The beautiful speeches

Toxic people have the language of a demon when it comes to persuading someone to do something they want. For some reason, they have this ability to spin words in a fabricated mess that seems almost too good to be true. They are among the most amazing liars, always testing the people around them to see who deserves their time.

Do not listen or let their persuasive words make you do something you do not want to do. Listen to your intuition and withdraw from any situation that makes you uncomfortable. They will try to manipulate you more if you don't.

4. Tirelessly needy

Toxic people will often start a discussion and a targeted dialogue with others only in order to speak about themselves. At the start of the conversation, they will make you feel like they are very interested in what is going on in your personal life but will always somehow turn the conversation around.

They will relentlessly flood you with the things they want. It is not just a general desire or need, and they will tell you exactly what they need from you or what they want you to do for them. Do not be easy prey to this manipulation.

5. Irregular body language and eye contact

While it can be very difficult for a liar to maintain eye contact with someone, they do everything they can to maintain proper body language and eye contact. To them, it makes them look like "normal" people with good intentions.

It couldn't be further from the truth. If you start to notice that they behave improperly, then chances are they want to get something from you. Don't be fooled, look them straight in the eyes, watch their hand movements to see if they are trying to cover their mouth or face. Sweating is a good clue, as well as the constant fluttering of the eyelids.

CHAPTER 11

HOW TO UNDERSTAND AN HONEST EMOTION VS A FAKE AND MANIPULATED EMOTION

It seems very simple to say, and the reality is that simple: When you feel good when you solve your problems easily, without drama, you are full of energy and vitality, and you feel optimistic ... then you are using authentic emotions.

An emotion is authentic when it responds to the stimulus that mobilizes it. This demolishes the terms "positive emotion" and "negative emotion" that have become obsolete when verifying that all emotions are necessary, and that fear or anger should not always be negative.

And what stimulus is it that mobilizes an emotion so that it is authentic?

First of all, each emotion must come into operation with a single stimulus. In this way, we will obtain the benefits of each one, and we will be able to verify that all the emotions, if used well, are fundamental for a life of well-being:

FEAR: Responds to the THREAT stimulus, and its objective is to set limits to any invasion or danger to obtain SECURITY. Ana was upset that her best friend calls her at any time regardless of her privacy; she began to feel angry and criticize her behind her back. Anger, in this case, would be a false emotion because the stimulus is threatening; with authentic fear, she would set limits asking for respect, and she would feel safer.

SADNESS: Responds to the stimulus of LOSS, and its objective is to think to solve and thus learn and DEVELOP. José left his partner; he was afraid of being alone and not finding another love story as beautiful as the one he lived, that had him distressed. Fear was a false emotion because what he suffered was a loss, not a threat. With sadness, he would accept and look for ways to improve from experience.

ANGER: Responds to the stimulus of LIE (manipulation, abuse, treason, injustice), and its objective is to take action to react and cut through deception to do JUSTICE. Eva suffered the betrayal of a colleague in her own business, and she felt sad because she did not expect such an outcome, so she felt guilty and did not raise her head. Sadness was a false emotion because we are talking about treason. With rage, she would have expressed herself and would have cut off the traitor, thus bringing justice to her life.

PRIDE: Responds to the stimulus of ADMIRATION, and its objective is to dare to value greatness in others and oneself, avoiding comparisons. Its purpose is RECOGNITION. Silvia was invited to participate in a Congress with a presentation, she began to feel fear, and this led her to feel inferior to the other speakers. Fear was a false emotion that weakened her. The right thing would have been to feel pride for the other speakers and also for herself, who had the opportunity to take a brave step towards her dreams.

LOVE: Responds to the stimulus of SAFE SPACE, and its objective is the dedication to everything worthwhile to achieve BELONGING with whomever one chooses. Marta dedicated herself to "saving" all the people she saw in need and then complained bitterly that she did not receive even a small part of what she gave. Here the false emotion is love because giving someone who only wants to take advantage is a threat, not a safe space. The real emotion would be to feel afraid and set limits when it comes to delivery.

JOY: Responds to the stimulus of UNEXPECTED GIFT, and its objective is to open up opportunities and flow with life in freedom to feel FULL. Manuel was a little curmudgeon, and it bothered him that his wife went to yoga and then stayed to have a beer with her friends. He saw it as unfair while he was bored alone at home. He felt false anger. The real thing would have been to connect with the joy of enjoyment and seek something pleasurable for him instead of angering the joy of others.

With these examples, you can see that all emotions can be very damaging when used with the wrong stimulus. Therefore, there are no positive or negative emotions, but authentic or false, that is, adequate or inadequately used. It is just a matter of re-learning their language, being alert to the stimulus, and using the correct emotion in each case.

A false emotion is ALWAYS accompanied by discomfort, negative energy, lack of vitality and enthusiasm. Also, problems that accumulate one after another, anxiety, stress, and other somatizations that produce emotional dysfunctions caused by the use of emotions that do not they respond to your stimulus.

Envy, resentment, feelings of guilt, interesting relationships, dependency, impotence, the feeling of inferiority, or superiority—all these are dysfunctions that are produced by using false emotions.

If you want your life to prosper, you have no choice but to manage your emotions. Otherwise, it will be your emotions that will direct your life, and you will be doomed to suffer one disaster after another.

CHAPTER 12

DETECTING DECEPTION, PROCEED WITH CAUTION

Do you think you are good at detecting when someone lies?

Maybe you are. Or maybe you think you are because, on average, we are only able to discover a lie in 54% of cases. Come on, throwing a coin in the air, we have almost the same probability of getting a head or a tail.

And so it is that many of the behaviors that are supposed to accompany a lie (avoid eye contact, get nervous, dilate the pupils, scratch the nose, etc.) can also appear in honest people who are simply shy or have a hard time in intense situations.

Below you'll find several myths about the science of lying that haven't proven useful.

1. Lying has its body language

Although the popular belief is that the body sends signals when we lie, no study has been able to relate a specific sign to deception.

Why? Because we all behave differently when lying, so do not believe that if someone does not look you directly in the eye or touch their face, they are deceiving you.

For every study that says liars scratch their noses, there is another that says otherwise. In an investigation, the gestures that appeared or disappeared when people lied were searched, but as you will see below, not enough differences were found to be able to generalize.

For example, people who lie stare in 67% of cases, but people who tell the truth also stare at 58%. There is no gesture that helps you accurately detect when you are being lied to.

2. Don't trust what they tell you

Although the widespread idea is that body language is more important than verbal language, that is also not true.

Body language may offer clues, but what is said may be even more reliable. In a 2004 study, a group of police officers watched a series of videos, and those who looked for inconsistencies in verbal cues (contradictions, doubts, etc.) were able to distinguish better lies than those who relied only on body signs (gaze direction, posture changes, etc.).

When you doubt if someone is telling you the truth or not, the most reliable thing is to find inconsistencies in their history. Later I will show you how.

3. The direction of the eyes gives clues

According to NLP (neurolinguistic programming), when someone moves his eyes to his right, it means he is lying, while if he moves his eyes to the left, he tells the truth.

If that were true, there would be no need to investigate further, and all liars would go with sunglasses, but it is false.

A 2012 study demonstrated that the direction in which someone looks is independent of the integrity of his story, so watch those gurus who promise PNL magical powers.

The people who lie the most do not look sideways or look away. If anything, they look at you more intently because they want to verify that you believe their lie.

4. The polygraph never fails

Another myth. As much as junk movies and television shows are trying to sell us the reliability of these devices, in one of the most rigorous studies, their percentage of success was established at only 65%. The main problem is its number of false positives: it often identifies people who are telling the truth as liars.

The reality is that detecting lies is VERY difficult. The reason is that most of us mix lie with true stories, which allows us to add real details that give more credibility.

Furthermore, each individual is so unique that there is no universal sign of lying. Not all of us have the same behavior when we lie: while I can avoid eye contact, maybe you will keep it.

It is for this reason that training to detect lies through the body or verbal language, has a success rate that reaches at most 60%, only 6 points more than without any preparation.

How do you know if a person is lying?

Below I will explain the exact tools to achieve this, but to start, you must be very clear about three fundamental concepts:

1. Look at the details and behavior changes

Simply paying attention to detail will do you better at spotting lies. It's that simple.

When someone lies, small differences may appear in their behavior or the story they are telling, and several studies have shown that focusing your attention on details will improve your ability to detect deception.

This is why women tend to be more skilled than men: they focus more on specific aspects of the stories and changes in behavior.

2. Try to isolate yourself from your emotions

I know it is complicated, but if you get angry, sad, or very happy, you will stop seeing those details.

When you are very emotional, your mind goes on automatic pilot. Disable some of its rational functions, and you will miss clues that could reveal that the other person is lying to you.

The most experienced liars want to do just that: put you in an altered state so that you stop asking questions and start making wrong decisions. So, keep a cool head and don't get excited by big promises or angry at huge suspicions.

3. In the end, you only have your instinct

The final step, once you have observed the details as coldly as possible, is to listen to your instincts.

Trust your intuition, because as it has been scientifically proven, we are more effective detecting lies when we do it unconsciously than if we try to tie all the ends rationally. The reason is that on an irrational level, you can see signs that your conscious mind overlooks.

So, pay attention, let some time pass, and be guided by your instinct. You will increase your chances of succeeding in detecting lies.

Although these three keys are essential, to have greater certainty that someone is lying to you, you need signs of deception, such as changes in behavior or contradictions in their history, to be evident.

CHAPTER 13

THE PSYCHOLOGY BEHIND READING BODY LANGUAGE

To know what people are like, you don't need long conversations, remember that words are blown away by the wind, so let's bet on something proven and scientifically supported: body language. Science has been commissioned to reveal some signs that will serve us well. You are going to learn the most important details of personality revealed by simple and common gestures.

This chapter will come in handy if you're dating someone, have a new coworker, or need to hire someone. Thanks to this guide, you will know how introverted, extroverted, selfish, or responsible a person can be. You don't need to listen to them, their body will speak for him or her.

1. How they smile and express their feelings

In a sincere smile, wrinkles appear near the lips and eyes, in a fake smile, only near the lips. When a person feels strong emotions, the eyes, nose, and mouth begin to swallow more frequently. If at least one of these factors is absent, emotions and feelings are not so sincere.

2. How they greet you

A strong and confident handshake indicates that in front of you is an outgoing person who likes to express their emotions. If in an encounter, he puts his hand on your shoulder, he is evaluating you, or there is a manipulator in front of you. If he takes you by the hand with two hands to greet you, your interlocutor prepared an order for you or wants to say something to you.

3. How often they check their mobile phone

The more the person updates their profile on their social networks, checks their mail or makes other movements with their mobile, the greater the probability that they are depressed and looking for encouragement outside.

4. How they take selfies

People who take selfies from below generally have a good attitude towards others. Those who are too serious and responsible rarely indicate their location and take photos in such a way that you will not know where they are. Meanwhile, excessive love for "duck faces" may indicate a high level of tension.

5. How they behave at the table

People who cut everything on their plate into small pieces are prone to long-term relationships and try to live by a plan. He who stirs even gastronomic masterpieces in a uniform mixture is strong, takes responsibility for many things, and usually does them. Those who eat very fast, are multifunctional, are respected at work, very rarely miss deadlines and think ahead. People who eat slowly, live in the present and know how to feel pleasure in life.

6. How they speak

If a person narrating a story often uses the word "I," he is most likely telling the truth. If this word is always present in their vocabulary, it may indicate that they are self-centered. Frequent use of "us" means that the person is social. Interestingly, with age, people use verbs less in the past tense and prefer to use them in the present tense.

7. How they eat popcorn

Research shows that introverts eat popcorn grain by grain and do so very carefully. Extroverts, in turn, love to grab a handful of popcorn and bring it directly to their mouths. Those who eat popcorn fast are less selfish and put the interests of others above their own.

8. Which coffee they prefer

Leaders prefer espresso, while double espresso is chosen by those who work under someone's direction. Latte lovers can sometimes experience difficulties with decision making and are slow by nature. Cappuccino is generally chosen by social and creative people, while those who prefer Frappuccino tend to be adventurous. Ordinary (American) black coffee is drunk by ordinary people who very rarely commit outlandish acts. Sugar and whipped cream are consumed by those who, from time to time, looking for new emotions, can do something extravagant.

9. Where they look while they drink

People who look at the depths of the cup from which they drink tea, or another beverage are generally more aware, focused, and tend to be idealistic. Those who look over the cup are more prone to influences from others, sometimes carefree, but at the same time, they feel better about the world around them. If someone drinks with their eyes closed, it means they feel some pain or discomfort and are looking for a way to relax.

CHAPTER 14

MASTERING THE SECRETS OF NON-VERBAL COMMUNICATION

Most people underestimate the role of facial expression and gestures in communication. But with the help of non-verbal signals, the first impression on the person is created. And they remember it for a long time. The gestures help or distract the listeners from the conversation, even if the lack of it brings information about the person speaking.

So, what do these or other gestures mean:

- the slow handshake speaks of a person's shyness and insecurity, and vice versa—a strong desire to impose his or her opinion.
- if a woman fixes her hair, it means that she moves.
- if one gestures with one hand only, it shows his unnaturalness.
- touching the forehead, mouth, nose is considered fraud.
- the crossing of arms speaks of skepticism and distrust of the interlocutor to the speaker.
- bent down, hunched over, shows low self-esteem and insecurity.

It is necessary to develop the observation in itself, as it helps to gather additional information about the people with whom the person should communicate.

Essential in the psychology of human behavior is the ability to listen and see. After all, the sound of the voice and its intonation, gestures and facial expressions of the interlocutor are of great importance.

How To Interpret Verbal Communication

Have you ever thought about evaluating your mode of communication? Do you use speech or gestures more to communicate with those around you? How do you define verbal communication? To help you to correctly distinguish between verbal communication, nonverbal communication, and visual communication, here's an overview of these topics...

Based on the findings of a study performed in 1967, the percentage distribution would be based on what is called the "3V rule." This rule states that the man communicates visually at a rate of 55%. For the rest: 38% communicate by voice and only 7% in verbal mode. Visual communication involves facial expressions and body language. Voice communication involves the sound of voice and intonation. But let's take a closer look at verbal communication.

Verbal communication definition

The first definition we give to verbal communication is the use of speech to communicate. For voice, quality is a criterion for analysis: speaking aloud, in a medium voice, in a slow voice, or a low voice... each style can considerably influence the type of message transmitted.

Another definition: verbal communication also designates all the means used to transmit elements of information. As its name suggests, the "verb" is very important in this form of communication. The verb is expressed by voice, but the lexical and auditory registers also come into play. The choice of words, as well as the quality of the voice, are all important indicators that make it easier to decipher a situation of communication, an emotion, or even a state of mind.

An example of original verbal communication? The language of monkeys used for communication with deaf people. Many people regularly doubt the famous 3V rule, and verbal communication could occupy more than this 7 %. This is a very important aspect of communication.

Verbal and non-verbal communication: the differences

To express we and transmit a message, several means of communication can be used. There are two very distinct modes of communication: verbal and non-verbal communication. How do you know if you use verbal communication rather than non-verbal communication when you speak to your colleagues, your employer, your colleagues, family, or friends? How to effectively distinguish verbal or non-verbal communication? The following will provide you with answers so that you can tell the difference between these two communication models.

One innate, the other involuntary

Verbal communication is acquired from birth (crying and shouting) while the different body languages (non-verbal) appear involuntarily, evolving with age and time. The learning of the use of verbs then begins at an early age by parents and teachers of primary school. For non-verbal communication, the evolution of the gestures continues autonomously and involuntarily.

Verbal and nonverbal are equally important

Communication by gestures, looks, posture, or expressions almost always accompanies words and voice. This means that verbal and non-verbal communication can be the subject of the same study.

Good point for non-verbal communication

To unmask a liar or to detect an attraction in a person, it would be better to focus on body language. The contradiction between gestures and speech could be much more frequent than the affirmation of the statement by body language...

The signs of the non-verbal

The list can be long, but here are a few: the smile (several types), the look, the color of the face, the hug, the grimaces, the position of the arms, the position of the hands and more...

Did you know that good verbal communication can contribute to personal development? So, if you want to decode verbal communication easily, you can read documents on verbal communication or follow a training dedicated to verbal communication.

CHAPTER 15

THE SUBCONSCIOUS MIND AND THE LIMBIC BRAIN SYSTEM

How do we make decisions that we practically don't think about? Is there an inherent part of the brain that leads us to decide without realizing it? According to the theory of the triune brain, it is like this:

The Three Brain Theory has shaped the popular imagination of brain function since the 1960s. This theory, also known as the "Triune Brain," was proposed by physicist and neuroscientist Paul MacLean. This theory is based on an idea; "three brains" can be identified in the human brain, which would have appeared at different evolutionary moments.

Reptilian brain (or R-Complex): It is the most instinctive and primitive part of the brain, located in the brainstem, diencephalon, and basal ganglia. With it, we make many of the unconscious decisions aimed at satisfying our most basic needs: reproduction, domination, self-defense, fear, hunger, flight, etc. Also, it is in charge of automatic processes, such as breathing and heart rate.

Paleo-mammal brain or limbic system: It is the part of the brain responsible for storing feelings and experiencing emotions, and, according to MacLean, it is observed in both mammals and birds. For this limbic system, there is only the binary: "pleasant" or "unpleasant."

Neo-mammalian brain or neocortex: It is the logical and rational, as well as the creative, part of our brain, typical of mammals and specially developed in the human species.

The success of the theory

The main advantage of this theory is its simplicity. However, this is the same thing that caused it to be discarded long ago from the academic field. Currently, it has been relegated to disciplines that are not fully developed in the field of neuroscience, such as neuromarketing or neuroeducation.

However, this simplicity in explaining the complex functioning of the brain has served to make it enormously popular, conquering the general public. The problem is that it has also allowed perpetuating a series of erroneous ideas or neuromites in popular knowledge and the disciplines named above.

"The triune brain theory is never mentioned in neuroscientific research, [it is] just a poetic and intuitive picture of how the brain has evolved and works in humans. Too bad it's not true, but it's not entirely bad either."

-Paul King-

The reptilian brain is not so reptilian

According to this theory, the brain is like an accumulation of layers that we have acquired throughout evolution as a species. However, the reality is that the brain did not evolve through further, one-way enhancement, as we would infer from the MacLean model. On the contrary, all the central circuits of the brain have been reorganized over time, causing some of them to expand and increase in complexity.

But also, the evolutionary stages do not coincide with those collected by MacLean. In essence, structures similar to the 'reptilian brain' are seen in fish and amphibians, and the reptiles themselves have a limbic system and simplified equivalents of our neocortex.

The reptilian brain is not guilty of unconscious decisions

If we do a little research on online consumption and neuromarketing, we will often come across references to MacLean's theory. From this area, the reptilian brain is considered the most important in unconscious decisions, such as consumer purchases. However, this discourse fails to attribute all unconscious decisions to the instincts of the 'reptilian brain,' even though structures of the limbic system (such as the amygdala) also participate in them.

The reality is that in humans, instinctive and emotional decisions are also powerfully influenced by the entire neocortex. Current studies, carried out with neuroimaging techniques, have determined that a highly distributed network makes most of the mental decisions of brain areas.

For example, research carried out a decade ago by neurologist John-Dylan Haynes revealed that our brain activity takes place up to 10 seconds before the participants in the experiment were aware of their own decisions. Furthermore, the curious thing is that most of this activity fell on the 'rational brain,' specifically in the prefrontal and parietal cortex. That means the decisions are not as "impulsive" or primitive as they may seem.

"Our" unconscious "decisions are predetermined long before our consciousness sets them in motion."

... Not even those related to consumption

We humans, as social animals, owe much of our evolutionary success to the fact that our cerebral cortex developed to allow us to relate to our fellow humans, through feelings of belonging. Thus, we socialize through behavior, often unconscious, of imitation (the first requirement for empathy).

Thus, it is not our deepest motivations that lead us to choose certain products, but our brain has been learning by imitation, or from experience itself. However, we

101

leave you a reflection: when we choose to get a coffee at a certain franchise or buy clothes in another, do we do it driven by a primary instinct, such as thirst or protection from the cold? Or because of a more complex drive to belong to a 'cool' brand or community?

CHAPTER 16

CHARACTERISTICS OR PROFILE OF AN ASSERTIVE AND NON-ASSERTIVE PERSON

The three different communication styles are passive, aggressive and assertive. The styles form a continuum, the passive and aggressive styles being the two extremes and the assertive style being the midpoint, that is, the optimum grade. Assertiveness is a way of communicating with others essential to have quality social relationships.

Assertiveness Characteristics

What is assertiveness? The definition of assertiveness consists of a set of practical social and communication skills. Assertive communication is based on respect for all parties and its objective is to negotiate an intermediate point between various positions. One of the most important characteristics of assertiveness and assertive attitude is the balance that it seeks and contributes to communication. Its benefits are remarkable, as they allow improving communication and maintaining healthier and more satisfying relationships. It also helps strengthen self-esteem, since self-respect is a basic pillar for assertiveness.

The assertiveness and assertive attitude are to express one's opinion and defend a point of view or some ideas taking into account the rights themselves, but also those of others. Respecting the point of view of the other, assertiveness promotes understanding and empathy and allows us to reach a common point.

Characteristics of an assertive person

People's communication fluctuates in this continuum depending on situations and circumstances, but they have a general tendency towards a communicative style. For example, assertive people can sometimes adopt a characteristic attitude of passive or aggressive communication style. However, they are categorized in the assertive communication style because they show a general tendency to relate with assertiveness. With the following description and the list of features, you can easily identify an assertive person.

Assertive person: definition

What is an assertive person? The Assertive people are those who practice an assertive communication style. Assertive behavior is based on respect for others and for oneself. Assertive people know their own rights and defend them, respecting others, that is, they will not "win," but "reach an agreement." They follow the method "I win, you win."

Assertive person: characteristics

What are the characteristics of an assertive person? The qualities of an assertive person are the following:

- **Speak calmly and directly**. In an assertive person, we can observe adequate fluidity, volume and speed, safety, direct eye contact, body relaxation, postural comfort and the absence of blockages or crutches. His facial expression is friendly, and he smiles frequently. He pauses and silences. He says what he means directly, knows how to make and receive compliments, and also asks and answers questions properly. His gestures are firm but not abrupt.

- **Express your thoughts and opinions**. The assertive person is able to express what he thinks, even though his opinions may differ from those of the rest. He can speak openly and honestly about his tastes and interests. He is able to express his disagreement with others and say "no."

- **Respect the opinions of others**. An assertive person knows how to accept their mistakes and respect the position of others, even if they do not share it.

- **Express your feelings**. Assertive people are able to express both positive and negative feelings.

- **Consider everyone's rights**. Assertive people know and believe in rights for themselves and for others. They defend their own, respecting those of others. They do not get too close to their interlocutor but respect their personal space.

- **Act adaptively**. The assertive person adapts to the context and acts in the most effective way in each situation.

- **Healthy self-esteem.** The assertive person does not feel inferior or superior to others, does not need to prove anything through aggressive communication. She feels good about herself and does not pretend to hurt others.

- **Communicate from serenity**. Another of the qualities of assertive people is that they speak from the calm and when the emotional intensity has decreased, producing the feeling of emotional control.

- **Goal is the midpoint**. An assertive person is not interested in getting what he wants at any price, but rather to reach an agreement between the two parties and that both benefits.

- **Satisfactory and fruitful interpersonal relationships**. Assertive people enjoy interpersonal relationships. Their way of communicating favors that they are well-valued by others and facilitates that they have a social support network.

Assertive person: examples

An example of a dialogue with an assertive person:

- Person 1: "Hello! Have you brought me the book I left you?"
- Person 2: "I have not brought it; I have forgotten again."
- Person 1: "I understand that you are busy with many things, but I need the book and many times you forget. How about I send you a message to remind you tomorrow?"
- Person 2: "Perfect!"

Characteristics of a non-assertive person: passive communication

A non-assertive person is the one who has a tendency to an assertive communication style, that is, passive or aggressive. Next, we will see in detail these communication styles.

Passive communication: characteristics

The characteristics of a passive person are as follows:

- **Speak little and low**. In a passive person, we can observe that he speaks with a low volume of voice and in a little fluid way. He presents blockages, stutters, hesitations, and silences. People with a passive communication style use

107

the words "maybe" and "I guess" a lot. They ask a few questions and answer with few words. They speak fast and unclear. They do not maintain eye contact, they have low eyes, tense faces, clenched teeth, trembling lips, nervous hands and tense and uncomfortable postures. They smile little and make nervous movements.

- **Do not express thoughts and opinions**. The passive person is not able to express what he thinks, especially if his opinions differ from those of the rest.

- **Put the opinions of others first**. A passive person respects the opinions of others and puts them before their own. Thus, they avoid disturbing or offending others. They are "sacrificial" people who live worried about satisfying others.

- **Do not express feelings.** Passive people often feel misunderstood, manipulated and disregarded, but they do not manifest it. So, they show emotional dishonesty. Although angry, they do not show anger or disagreement, they do not express their true feelings. In the following paragraph, you will find why it is so difficult to express feelings.

- **Take into account the rights of others**. Passive people put the rights of others before considering their own. They respect others scrupulously but do not respect themselves.

- **Act from fear**. The passive person feels insecure and does not want to disturb others.
- **Low self-esteem**. The passive person has low self-esteem, does not feel good about herself and therefore needs to be loved and appreciated by everyone. Consequently, they act to please others.
- **Hold others accountable**. Passive people frequently complain about others: "X doesn't understand me," "Y is an egoist and takes advantage of me," and so on.
- **Goal is not to get angry**. A passive person is terrified of conflicts, does not know how to deal with disagreement with others and is unable to think about the possibility of facing someone. Therefore, they prioritize the opinions and wishes of others at any price.
- **Insane interpersonal relationships**. Passive people cannot enjoy social relationships. Maintaining this communicative style causes frequent feelings of anxiety, frustration, sadness and helplessness.

Passive communication: example

An example of habitual responses by a passive person is as follows:

- Person 1: "Hello! Have you brought me the book I left you?"

- Person 2: "I have not brought it; I have forgotten again."
- Person 1: "Well, nothing happens, it doesn't matter."
- Person 2: "It doesn't bother you, right?"
- Person 1: "Well, I needed it today, but it's the same thing."
- Person 2: "Well, I'll bring it to you tomorrow, okay?"
- Person 1: "Okay."

Characteristics of a non-assertive person: aggressive communication

Non-assertive people are those who tend to behave passively or aggressively. The aggressive communication style is the opposite of the passive, it is the other end of the continuum. At both ends, the ideal would be to work social skills to get closer to the center.

Aggressive communication: features

The characteristics of an aggressive person are the following:

- **Talk a lot and loud.** In an aggressive person, we can observe that he speaks with a high volume of voice, fast and emphatically. He uses imperatives and derogatory language with foul words and even insults and threats. He throws many linked questions and answers quickly. A challenging attitude is perceived in eye contact. He usually shows his face and tense hands and adopts a body posture that invades the personal space of the interlocutor, so that he feels invaded and intimidated. He also gestures with threatening movements.

- **Express thoughts and opinions without filter.** The aggressive person expresses what he thinks and believes without taking into account the feelings of others.

- **Put your opinions and wishes first.** An aggressive person expresses their wishes and opinions as the only valid options. They do not respect the opinions of others. Sometimes, they don't even allow them to express these opinions.

- **Express emotions uncontrollably.** Aggressive people often have sudden excessive outbursts of aggression. These outbursts are usually quite uncontrolled, as they are the result of an accumulation of tensions and hostility. They lack social skills to regulate their expression.

- **Do not take into account the rights of others.** Aggressive people defend their interests without respecting the rights of others.

- **Act from fear.** The aggressive person thinks that if they do not behave in this way, they are excessively vulnerable.

- **Low self-esteem.** The aggressive person does not feel good about themselves and therefore needs to be respected by others, defend themselves by attacking and "winning" the other in communication.
- **Do not listen.** The aggressive person communicates unidirectionally, does not listen and has an attitude of contempt for others.
- **Goal is to win.** An aggressive person cannot stand that things do not go as they want. They think that the important thing is to get what they want at any price.
- **Insane interpersonal relationships.** It is complicated to deal with aggressive people and cause rejection in others. So, they may feel lonely, frustrated, misunderstood and guilty. Their attitude of contempt and disrespect can generate great conflicts in their interpersonal relationships.

Aggressive communication: example

An example of a dialogue with an aggressive person is as follows:

- Person 1: "Hello! Have you brought the book I left you?"
- Person 2: "I didn't bring it, I forgot it again."
- Person 1: "But it's the fourth time you are forgetting it!"

- Person 2: "I was going to take it, but in the end I forgot."
- Person 1: "It's always the same, you don't remember anything. I want it right now. "

HOW TO LEARN TO BE ASSERTIVE

How to learn to be assertive with positive communication? Assertive communication opens doors in your life, since, through this experience, you have the ability to express your opinions and points of view while respecting your rights, but also those of people around you. There is an interpersonal relationship scheme that can help you to walk in the direction of assertiveness: "I am fine, you are fine." That is, position yourself in a framework of reality in which two people relate from interpersonal equality.

Express your opinions to be assertive

You are a unique and irreplaceable person. You can bring your own essence to others. Therefore, value your own voice and your views. It is not about imposing your opinions but expressing them naturally. Sometimes people avoid showing their opinions for fear of conflict.

If you have ever felt this way, then start taking the initiative to show your opinions in simple and concrete actions. For example, if you go to the movies with your group of friends, express clearly which movies you are especially interested in and which ones you don't want to watch.

Learn to say no to gain assertiveness

How many times do you suffer from your own internal contradictions by saying yes to something you really wanted to say no to? "No" is a short word, however, it produces such a psychological impact on the mind of the person who pronounces this message that, when a person has a low level of assertiveness, he suffers when setting limits.

Remember that when you say no to someone else's request, you are not rejecting that person, you are simply putting into practice your ability to decide. Stop justifying yourself for everything as if you really had to. Language is rich and broad. Therefore, use it to open doors.

How to learn to be assertive in practice?

Imagine that a friend wants to talk to you today to tell you about an important issue, but you had a horrible day and you don't have a good disposition to really focus on that conversation. In that case, you can express an assertive message of this type: "Thank you very much for sharing with me what has happened to you. Today I had a bad day and I am very tired. If you think it's a good idea too, we can talk tomorrow. Then, I can give you the time and attention you deserve. "

Too often, we move in a narrow frame of closed questions that only admit the answer to "yes" or "no." However, it is important that you make positive use of language to use it in its full range of nuances.

Defend your rights

Another secret to being more assertive is to express messages in the first person. For example, imagine that you often get angry at a friend because he arrives late for plans and you always have to wait. In that case, a frequent mistake is to fall into reproach through messages such as "you are unpunctual."

To gain assertiveness, try to express your requests following the essence of "I." For example, you can express this idea: "When you're late for our plans, I feel you don't value my time and that makes me feel sad." When we express an idea in the first person, we awaken more empathy in the other. That is, assertiveness invites understanding.

Although language opens doors when used correctly, remember that you don't just express a message through words. It is important that your tone of voice is also aligned with the verbal message and body language information. Currently, there are many different means of communication. However, if you have to address an important issue, it is better to talk with that person face to face, since eye contact creates a climate of emotional confidence.

Assertive Words

Another of the best techniques to be assertive is to take care of your communication: "Thank you," "I'm sorry," "I love you" and "please." Beautiful, simple and constructive words that, used in the right context, are a clear example of assertiveness. That is, do not hesitate to apologize if you were wrong. Appreciate the beautiful gestures that other people have with you in your daily routine.

Express your feelings of affection with freedom and naturalness. At work, remember that the formula "please" generates empathy and kindness. Language builds your reality. Therefore, try to make your words positive and kind.

CHAPTER 17

SENSING LIES

Can we tell if someone is lying by just observing their body language? Do our gestures and behaviors give us away? It is not always easy to know when the person in front of us is lying to us. We all remember the children's story of "Pinocchio," the boy whose nose grew more and more every time he told a lie.

Although in real life it is not always so obvious to guess lies, some experts help us solve this dilemma. That is, they show us the situations most prone to our body language giving us away. Thus, lies can not only be detected through spoken language. Observing those around us and studying their body language will allow us to discover people who are not being honest with us.

90% of our communication is a non-verbal language. Therefore, our body says much more about us than we can express in words.

On the other hand, the truth is that we began to lie at a very early age. Lying is a behavior learned and intrinsic to the human being. If the young child ends up learning that the reward for lying is greater than that obtained by telling the truth, it is normal for him to risk delving a little deeper into that world of what has been invented, which produces so many benefits.

Saying you're sick the day of an exam you haven't studied for, bragging about knowing a language when, in fact, you can barely understand it, attributing the delay to traffic— these are behaviors that we carry out every day, with total naturalness.

Five Gestures of Our Body Language That Give Us Away

The more we study the body language of those around us, the better positioned we will be to perceive the gestures that accompany their lies. Although there is no universal signal to detect lies, among the most common are these five:

The tendency to scratch your nose

A person who is lying tends to rub their nose involuntarily and reflexively. The explanation for this gesture is that the increased adrenaline secreted after the lying behavior causes itchiness when reaching the nasal capillaries.

The most famous example is that of Bill Clinton: he rubbed his nose when he denied his affair with Monica Lewinsky. Then it was interpreted as a sign that he was not telling the truth.

Body in a rigid position

The muscles tend to tense, and this causes the inability to control some tics, such as the contraction of the shoulders or small spasms in the feet and neck. Physical expression is limited, with a tendency to stick the arms to the body.

On the other hand, when the person is sincere, the most natural thing is for them to be relaxed, their gestures are reassuring, and they show relaxed body language. However, be careful when interpreting this rigidity: the tension may be derived from other circumstances. Either a concern that has nothing to do with what they are saying or the anticipation of our reaction when sharing the truth.

Breathing and heart rate accelerates

The respiratory rate changes, you breathe more heavily. This causes the heart rate to change due to an abruptly altered respiratory rate. In this case, it would be good to also take into account what we have indicated for body stiffness.

Static look

Holding your gaze is emotional protection. When we lie, we put ourselves in a position of conscious vulnerability. Once said, the doubt can betray us; hence the rigidity in

119

the discourse usually moves to the body, and logically, to our gaze.

Facial micro expressions

The blinking becomes more intense and frequent, with a tendency to rub our eyes. The cheeks begin to blush as a result of the increased adrenaline, and the mouth and lips pucker, indicating increased emotional tension.

The causes for which we lie can be many and very diverse, but they all have a common objective: we want to avoid telling the truth.

Evidence of body language

Body language is a form of non-verbal communication. Through gestures and movements, we transmit the messages that we want to send to our interlocutors. These actions are usually carried out unconsciously, that is why it is so difficult to plot a lie and for our body gestures to be consistent with what we want to express. Our body accompanies our speech in the same way as when telling the truth.

On the other hand, as we have said, the interpretation of non-verbal language must be made with caution, since there is a multitude of environmental factors that can influence it. Imagine that you observe in your interlocutor an excess of sweat on the forehead, you do not have to interpret it as a sign that he is trying to lie to you. It may be that the room is excessively hot or he has hyperhidrosis.

To interpret non-verbal language, it is necessary to take into account the variables of the context, the person's background, his character, and the significance of what he is sharing through his speech. Ideally, look at body language as a whole and rule out possible external factors that may explain behavior and have nothing to do with lying.

"Telling the truth can be done by an idiot. To lie takes imagination."

-Perich-

CHAPTER 18

FAKE YOUR BODY LANGUAGE AND MANIPULATE ANYONE'S

Your body language can influence how people perceive you. Your position, your tone of voice, and your gestures influence the opinion that others have of you.

According to Mark Bowden, an expert in non-verbal language, this opinion counts for more than one would think.

Here are some basic techniques that will help you fake your body language well, and thus ensure that your message is received.

1. Hands down for confidence. Place your hands at navel level on the Truth Plane. It is an imaginary place on your body, a horizontal plane that extends 180 degrees from the navel.

If you put your hands on it while you speak, you will start to feel more confident, more balanced, and more present. As a result, the people who look at you will perceive you to be more honest and trustworthy.

For example, look at newsreaders. These, often trained by people like Mark Bowden, will mainly have their hands in this position, whether sitting or standing. They place their hands at the level of the Truth Plane because the audience thus feels more confident.

2. Hands up for passion. Bring your hands up to your chest, what Mark Bowden calls the plane of passion. No matter what you do, keep your hands constantly above chest level.

In this way, your heart rate and the rate of your breathing increase, just like those of your audience. So, you can excite an audience just by bringing your hands into the plane of passion.

3. Sitting. If you sit at a table and put your hands on your face, no one will be able to see your lips. However, we read a lot more on the lips than we think. As a result, people will think that you are trying to hide something, and no one will believe what you are saying.

In meetings, people often sit very close to the table to protect themselves. It is a mistake. You must position yourself so that people can see your body more. The more people can see your body, the more confident they feel. So, sit down, move your chest back about a foot from the table if you want to look calm and confident, and place your hands at navel level.

4. Standing. When giving a presentation, do not stand behind the podium, as no one can see your body. So they can't tell how you are feeling. The mind will then tend to go towards the negative.

Get out of this position and show yourself more. Use positive body language, and people's reaction to you will be positive.

5. Don'ts. Communicating is often stressful, especially in front of an audience or with your boss. The worst mistake people make is to hang their arms on the side of the body. This position, which shows signs of anxiety, is the one you will tend to take when you want to escape or attack.

Look at the great world leaders and note where their hands are. Are they on either side of the body, in the navel area, or the passion area? Have you ever seen them talking with their hands covering their faces?

6. To do. To show leadership, you want people to trust you. So, clear your stomach, put your hands on the Truth Plane, and you will build confidence. The tone is also important. Your body language changes your voice intonation, positive or negative. When your hands reach the passion zone, located at the chest level, the intonation of your voice increases at the end of each sentence, and this, naturally. This inflection is a universal sign that says something will happen next.

CHAPTER 19

HOW TO INFLUENCE AND SUBDUE ANYONE'S MIND

Mind control techniques do exist and, depending on their use, can be very flattering or counterproductive. Mind control has many meanings, so that it can be confusing. It can be known as coercive persuasion, brainwashing, thought reform, manipulation, among others.

All of these names share elements in common, elements that define mind control. All refer to the persuasion and direct or indirect influence of the mind of an individual to fulfill a task. Next, we will define mental control, specifying some of its techniques. Also, we will make clear who uses this type of mind control techniques and what their benefits are, both positive and negative.

What is mind control?

Under the umbrella of mind control are a series of techniques aimed at mastering and modifying the mental processes of an individual. These kinds of mind control techniques are no fantasy; in many cases, they are very effective and, in certain cases, irreversible. Despite this, not all mind control is necessarily negative, since there are beneficial uses.

125

Mind control techniques can have very powerful effects. They can significantly influence an individual, in their actions, behaviors, thoughts, beliefs, tastes, relationships, and even in their own identity.

Researcher Steve Hassan makes a distinction between mind control and brainwashing. The distinction is in the awareness of being manipulated or influenced. In brainwashing, the victim knows that she is being manipulated so that her thoughts change in favor of the aggressor. Whereas, in mind control, the person does not have to be aware of the manipulation of which he is being victimized.

In this sense, mind control can be very subtle and sophisticated. Something that makes it dangerous, even when done with good intentions. Because someone, through mind control, can change the way of being of other people without them knowing. The manipulator can be anyone, even someone very close.

Some mind control techniques

These mind control techniques are subtle and slow; that is, they do not have an immediate effect. Mind control is a long process, which changes the mind of the manipulated gradually. However, this depends a lot on the techniques used, the duration of the application, and the personal and social factors of the manipulated.

Furthermore, in applying mind control techniques, physical strength is not necessary. However, there is great psychological and social pressure on the manipulated. Anyone is susceptible to mind control. That is where the danger lies in the misuse of these kinds of mental manipulations.

Some of the best known and most effective mind control techniques are:

- **Total or partial isolation from the family or social nucleus.** Cutting the affective ties of the possible manipulated person facilitates the process of mental control, since there is total or partial dependence on the manipulator.

- **Gradual physical exhaustion.** Various activities are used to decrease the physical and cognitive abilities of the manipulated—for example, forced labor or excessively long working days.

- **Diet change.** An abrupt change in diet, especially decreasing protein, also weakens the body and mind of the victim.

- **The constant reminder of simple or complex ideas.** It is one of the most critical methods because it would be successful in mind-control, only holding in mind continuously the thoughts that want to be put into the controlled. This can be done orally, with chants and mantras, or with signs and reading provided in writing.

- **Measured displays of rewards and love.** The manipulator gives the manipulated attention and incentives as long as the manipulator does something that encourages manipulation of the mind—all of this to establish a connection between the abuser and the manipulator.

- **Subtle or direct use of drugs.** The use of narcotics is not mandatory, but it does facilitate mind control.

- **Hypnosis.** To make vulnerable the mind of the manipulated, and in this way, facilitate the manipulation process itself.

Who uses these mind control techniques?

Mind control can be used by anyone who wants to manipulate or influence another individual. Furthermore, those who use these techniques have very specific purposes, which can be political, social, and personal because they seek an individual to lose his freedom of thought and personal peculiarities.

Therefore, mind control is generally employed by cults or sects. It is used to add new followers and keep members active by the leaders of the sects or cult who use the mental techniques on their followers.

Also, mind control techniques can be used by people with a low degree of empathy to manipulate and exploit another person. However, there can also be some mental control present between intimate relationships in which one of the parties abuses his/her power. As, for example, in relationships of teacher/student, parents/children, boss/subordinate, doctor/patient, among others.

The usefulness of mind control techniques

Not all applications of these mind control techniques have a negative connotation. They can also be beneficial in certain circumstances, as long as they are not invasive or imposed.

When mindful doctors or psychologists use these mind control techniques, it can be extremely beneficial in the lives of certain patients. It can be used to suppress an addiction, overcome a traumatic experience, improve self-esteem, and even eliminate suicidal or self-destructive thoughts. Ultimately, mind control techniques are not bad in and of themselves, and they are only bad when used for evil purposes.

Tricks to Influence And Subdue People's Mind

Before you begin, it is important to note that none of these methods are intended to influence other people with obscure intent. Anything that could be harmful to someone in any way, especially their self-esteem, is not included here. These are ways to make friends and influence people using psychology in a positive way and without making someone feel bad.

1. Benjamin Franklin effect

Getting someone to do us a favor can be tricky, and this is also known as the Benjamin Franklin effect. Legend has it that when Franklin was in the Pennsylvania Legislative Assembly, there was an opponent who had once spoken against him (Franklin does not say his name), someone very influential. Franklin was very uneasy about this opposition and hatred and decided to win over this gentleman. What occurred to him is very curious and intelligent. Instead of doing that gentleman a favor or service, he induced the opponent to do him a favor by borrowing a very rare book from his library. The gentleman in question lent it to him immediately, and Franklin returned it after a week with a note in which he greatly appreciated the favor. When they met again in parliament, the gentleman spoke to him (which he had never done before) and, above all, with a great education. From then on, this gentleman was always ready to help Franklin, and they became great friends, a friendship that continued until his death. This fact demonstrates the truth of a maxim that Franklin had learned as a child that says: "It is more likely that someone who has already done a previous one will do you another favor rather than one who owes it to you."

There is another striking example of this phenomenon in The Brothers Karamazov by Dostoyevsky. Fyodor

Pavlovitch recalls how, once in the past, he was asked why he had hated a person so much. And he answered them: "I will tell you. He has done me no harm. I was very dirty with him once and have hated him ever since." Just as in these examples, we obtain a vicious circle, the Benjamin Franklin effect shows that it is also possible to generate virtuous circles.

The scientists decided to test this theory and found that those who were asked by the researcher for a personal favor, made much more favorable assessments of him than the other groups. It may seem contradictory since common sense tells us that we do favors for people we like, and we annoy those we don't like. But the reality seems to be that we tend to like people with whom we are kind and to dislike people with whom we are rude or misbehave ourselves.

2. Too many

At first, the trick is to ask for much more than we want or need, and later to lower our demand. You start by reaching anyone with a very inflated request, and the request is most likely to be denied. And, shortly after, you turn around and think about something less excessive, which is really what you wanted in the first place. This trick might also sound counter-intuitive, but the theory behind it is that the individual feels bad for refusing our first request, even though it was not fair, so when we ask for anything rational, they feel more inclined to help this time.

3. The name it deserves

Depending on the case, using a person's name or title is another confidence-building device. It is extremely necessary and successful to make friends by using someone's name. The name of a person is said to be the sweetest sound for that person in any language. The name is the fundamental part of our identity, so listening to it validates our life and leads us to feel more optimistic about the individual who validates us. Using a title or nickname can have very strong effects too. This can be as easy as calling an acquaintance "mate" or "partner" whenever we see him, or referring to a person we choose to work with or continue to work with as a "boss." While this might sound corny, it works in practice.

4. Flattery

Flattery opens many doors. This may seem obvious at first, but there are some important caveats to be aware of. For starters, it is important to know that if flattery is not seen as sincere, it will do more harm than good. Researchers have studied the motivations and reactions behind flattery and have found some very important things. People tend to seek cognitive balance, always trying to keep their thoughts and feelings organized similarly. So, if we flatter someone who has high self-esteem and finds it sincere, they are going to like it very much, as we are validating their feelings. However, if we flatter someone who has low self-esteem, there is a chance that it could backfire, because it interferes with how it is perceived. That does not, of course, mean we should degrade a low self-esteem person.

5. Mirroring or the mirror technique

Mirroring, also known as mimicry or mirror technique, is something that some people do naturally. People with this ability are considered "chameleons"; They try to fit in with their surroundings by copying the attitudes, movements, and even speech patterns of other people. This ability, however, can also be used consciously and is a great technique for becoming more friendly. The researchers studied mimicry and found that those who had been imitated were much more likely to act favorably towards the person who had copied them. Even more interesting was their second finding, that those with someone who imitated their behavior seemed more interesting and more personable in front of others. The reason this is likely is that the reflection of someone's behavior makes them feel validated. This validation is positively associated with feeling greater self-esteem and greater security, more happiness, and feeling a better disposition towards others.

6. The use of fatigue

People are more sensitive to something when they are exhausted, so someone will tell them whether it's a comment or a question. The explanation for this is that their mental energy levels drop significantly when they are tired. When we ask someone who is tired a question, they will probably not have a definitive answer, and we will probably get an "I will do it tomorrow" answer because they do not want to face the decisions at that moment. The next day, they are more likely to help us, as people tend to keep their word; it is psychologically natural to want to go ahead with something you said would be done.

7. Offers that cannot be rejected

It consists of starting with a request that they cannot reject. This is a reverse "aim high" technique. Instead of starting with a large order, you start with something very small. Once someone has agreed to help us or agrees with us, they will be more likely to be more receptive to fulfilling a larger request. Scientists tested this phenomenon in advertising. They started by getting people to express their support for the environment and rain forests, which is a fairly simple request. Next, they found that once someone had come to express their agreement to support the environment, it was much easier to convince them to buy products that supported rainforests and whatnot.

8. Know how to correct

Correcting people when they are wrong isn't a smart idea. Carnegie also pointed out in his popular book that it is basically needless to tell others they're wrong to get them to stay away from us. There is a better way to show disagreement and turn it into a polite conversation without telling them that they are wrong, as it affects the essence of their ego. The idea behind this is quite simple: instead of arguing, listen to what they have to say and then try to understand how they feel and why. Then discover the common ground that you share with them and use it as a starting point to explain your position. This makes the other person much more likely to listen to what you have to say and allow you to correct him without losing your position.

9. Repeat things

Repeating something that our interlocutor has just said is one of the most positive ways to influence others, since we show that we understand what they are saying to us and how they feel, thus manifesting our empathy. One of the most effective ways to do this is to paraphrase what they say and repeat it, also known as reflective listening. Studies have shown that when therapists use reflective listening, people tend to reveal their emotions more and have a better therapeutic relationship. This can be transferred by talking to our friends. If we listen to what they tell us and rephrase it as a question to confirm that we understand it, they will feel more comfortable talking to us. They are also going to show more friendship and will be more likely to listen to what we have to say, as it showed that we care about them.

10. To agree

While talking, nod, particularly when you want to ask for a favor. Scientists have found that people are more likely to agree with the other person when they nod while listening to something. They have also seen that when someone nods a lot in front of us, we end up doing the same. This is understandable because human beings are well known for imitating behaviors, especially those that we consider having a positive connotation. So, if you want to be very convincing, nod regularly throughout the conversation. The person who is speaking will find it difficult not to agree, and they will begin to feel good vibrations towards what is being said, without even knowing it.

CHAPTER 20

SUBLIMINAL MESSAGES

The first step that we are going to take before establishing the meaning of the term "subliminal message" is to know the etymological origin of the two words that shape it:

- Message emanates from the Provençal "message," which, in turn, comes from the ancient Latin verb "Mittere," which can be translated as "command."
- Subliminal, meanwhile, has its origin in Latin and comes to mean "what is below consciousness." It is a word made up of the following parts: the prefix "sub-," which is synonymous with "below"; the noun "limits," which is equivalent to "limit"; and the suffix "-al," which is used to indicate that something is "relative to."

The message is the communication entity. This is the material that transmits information consisting of signs, symbols, or signals. Therefore, the contact cycle requires the involvement of a sender, who transmits a message to one or more receivers via a medium or channel.

Subliminal, on the other hand, is a term used in psychology to explain what is below the consciousness level. As the term is applied to a stimulus, it refers to the fact that it is not perceived consciously due to its brevity or weakness, though it affects behavior.

Therefore, the definition of subliminal messaging refers to a message intended to be conveyed below normal vision limits. This message hits the receiver but is not intentionally received by the receiver. This may be a sound or picture that the receiver unconsciously perceives and may alter his actions in this absence of a conscious mechanism.

Within the field of music, it has been discovered that there are also subliminal messages. Specifically, scholars have discovered that these have been achieved through a technique called backmasking, which originated in the 1960s. This, which consists of recording backward, has hidden messages for different purposes.

In the world of cinema, there are also considered to be many subliminal messages. An example is animation films that come out of the Disney factory or Pixar, and that are mainly aimed at children.

Thus, for example, in the films of the last production company, "A113" usually appears. This combination of letters and numbers becomes the identification of the classroom in which the current Pixar leaders studied and learned everything they know about animation.

There is a consensus among psychologists about the existence and capacity of subliminal messages to generate effects on the receptors. Experts argue, however, that its consequences on people's behavior are neither long-lasting nor powerful.

Subliminal messages are prevalent in advertising, whether in advertisements for companies that want to increase sales or in advertisements for governments that want to influence the population subtly.

Techniques for Embedding Subliminal Messages

One of the techniques uses sounds below the audible level to disguise sound messages between music, behind spoken communication, or through even more sophisticated techniques.

Large stores or supermarket networks may be using those sounds or messages behind the background music.

They can also use jingles, which, according to the dictionary, are "musicalized advertising messages, consisting of simple short choruses, specific to be remembered and hummed easily."

In a short time, they end up permeating the mind, subconscious to people with their subliminal inductions.

One of the recommended intentions for its use is to prevent theft; however, the actual intention is much more insidious than that, apparently.

Commands like obey - buy more - spend - sleep - we are watching you, can be repeated countless times, in a rhythmic and monotonous voice, in very low volume.

They are introduced directly into the subconscious, to circumvent the defense mechanisms of the conscious mind.

The subconscious, then, is forced to produce command-induced sensations and stops creating the state of alert, which makes us more attentive to something that may be wrong.

As it can be seen, the intention of the subliminal message is not to manipulate the conscious, but to stimulate feelings and sensations, such as fear - hate - love - euphoria - torpor, induced by the commands.

And, most serious, is that the message can also produce altered states of consciousness.

Dick Sutphen, a theosophist, and student of hypnosis and related states, relates an experience of subliminal manipulation, in which he participated: "I went with a group to a meeting in a Los Angeles auditorium where more than ten thousand people gathered to listen to a charismatic figure.

About twenty minutes after I arrived, I sensed that he was entering an altered state of consciousness and leaving it. Those who accompanied me experienced the same.

Due to our careful observation, we perceived what was happening, but those around us did not perceive anything.

What appeared to be a spontaneous demonstration was, in fact, cunning manipulation."

According to him, group trance induction, in this case, was due to a vibration of six to seven cycles per second that sounded along with the sound of the air conditioning.

That particular vibration generates alpha rhythms that leave people extremely susceptible to suggestion.

Almost a third of the global population is capable of entering such states. Another subliminal manipulation technique is "stuffing."

In this, the visual messages are hidden between the frames and are projected so fast that they cannot be seen.

It consists of printing commands in a faint and almost erased way in the background of printed boxes.

The result is practically invisible to the eyes. Computers today do this quickly and automatically.

They print a background mosaic with words like sleep, obey, sex, etc., messages that no one notices.

Printed matter, such as newspapers, magazines, adult and children's books, may contain written messages, images, and symbols embedded in the background.

In this way, the hidden and repeated messages weaken the subconscious, which would alert us to hidden commands.

The drawing technique is the most common of the subliminal messages.

Television

TV does much more than entertain, and it is also capable of producing altered states of consciousness.

In these, the person uses the right hemisphere of the brain more, where opiate neurotransmitters–endorphins–are released, substances chemically almost identical to opium. Under its effects, the person experiences pleasant sensations and will always want to repeat them.

Research by H. Krugman shows that while people watch television, the activity of the right hemisphere of the brain exceeds that of the left in a ratio of two to one.

This means that influenced by TV, people begin to present altered states of consciousness AND are often in a trance state, as TV provides them with their "fixed dose" of opiate endorphins.

To measure the attention and wakefulness of people in front of the television, psychologist Thomas Mulholland carried out the following experiment: He connected young television viewers to electroencephalography devices.

The device was connected to a cable that interrupted transmission whenever the youngsters' brain activity produced an increase in alpha waves.

Although asked to focus on what was being displayed, only a few managed to keep the device connected for more than 30 seconds!

Many viewers already live hypnotized, and it is very easy to deepen their trance state.

The simplest way is to insert a black frame every thirty-two frames in the film.

This creates a pulse of forty-five pulses per minute that only the subconscious perceives, and this is the ideal rhythm to provoke deep hypnosis.

Until the age of sixteen, children will have spent more than fifteen thousand hours watching TV, much more time than they spend at school.

A television, on average, stays connected almost seven hours a day in a normal house, according to statistics from the 1980s, and this increased.

Today, many people are rapidly heading towards a world in an "alpha state": placid and glassy gaze, and prompt and obedient response to instructions and commands.

Suppose a movie shows sixty frames per second, and our perception registers just forty-five per second. If a bottle of a soda is projected on one of these, the conscious will not notice it, but the subconscious will.

If screened five or six times during the movie, the person may suddenly feel an uncontrollable and unconscious desire to drink soda, even if they are not in the habit of drinking it or it is not their favorite!

An experiment was carried out in the United States to test the efficacy of this technique. In a film, the message "eat popcorn," which in Spanish means "coma pochoclo," was projected several times in rapid flashes.

At the exit of the cinema, a cart of popcorn was placed, and the line to buy them reached the other corner.

A third and effective technique of subliminal manipulation is that of "masking," in which subliminal messages are cleverly incorporated into printed material (pictures, drawings) or engraving.

Brain Wash

When you start putting subliminal messages behind the music together, to project subliminal scenes on a screen, produce hypnotic visual effects, and hear musical rhythms that induce a trance state, you get extremely effective brainwashing.

CHAPTER 21

ARE YOU A VISUAL, KINESTHETIC, OR AUDITORY PERSON?

You may present the characteristics of each of these dimensions, but do not identify yourself with one in particular. Our way of being is linked to our senses.

As you may already know, humans have five senses that connect them to the world around them: olfactory, gustatory, tactile, visual, and auditory. But in general, each of us tends to use a particular sense to interact with the world. So it is interesting to know what type of person you are, a visual person, for example.

And you, how do you interact with the world?

This theory is evoked by Neurolinguistic Programming, saying that the world in which we live is perceived differently by each person. Indeed, each of us uses different senses, the most related to our personality.

It is an interesting point of view that it is worth taking into account to get a little better understanding of us. You will use one or two senses, far more than the other three.

It is also fascinating to learn that this perception has to do with our cognitive predominance; that is, some people use the left side much more than the right side, and vice versa. For example, people who use the left-hand side more are borrowed more from logic and concerned with order.

Conversely, if you use a lot more of the right part, you would be more creative, more versatile, and more innovative.

Neurolinguistic psychology then deals with understanding which brain areas we use the most to determine how we perceive the world around us.

Do you want to know what your innate inclination is? Then read this section to find out whether you are a person with visual, kinesthetic, or hearing.

1. A visual person

Are you one of the people who must read or study in absolute silence? This is something very common among visual people who then need silence to be able to concentrate.

It is also possible that when you are driving while listening to music, you may have to turn off the radio if you start looking for a particular street or place to stay focused.

They are people who are usually very active and observant. They have a sense of detail and let nothing that attracts appearance pass by. It is easier for them to memorize images. These people generally like parks or forests to relax.

2. Auditory people

Are you one of those people who think aloud often? You may surprise many people with this rather curious habit, but in reality, you are one of the hearing people.

You then appear to verbalize a lot, to the point that you speak to yourself. It's also very normal that if you're an audible person, you enjoy listening to others because that's how you memorize things: by listening to them loudly and rarely in writing.

They are also very articulate people who have a good sense of communication, know how to express themselves very well, and enjoy listening to others. Nothing surprises them, and they will pursue a conversation while listening to music at the same time.

A ton of stuff they can do at the same time, unlike visual people who often have difficulty focusing because they are constantly distracted by several items.

3. Kinesthetic people

Do you like manual work? Cooking, building, working

outdoors, planting, cultivating, growing plants? Are you one of the people who do a lot of sport? Then you are possibly a kinesthetic person.

Neurolinguistic psychology indicates that kinesthetic people, in addition to being fairly worried, have a particular taste for emotions and for everything that has to do with physical and manual things.

They are among the people who like to experience things for themselves rather than hearing about them. They like, for example, to express their feelings by taking people in their arms, by caressing them, or even by eating a meal.

They are intimate and tactile people who, as visual people can be, usually do not have a strong interest in the information. They're much more spontaneous in introspection or reflection.

To conclude, we may assume that you might have a percentage of every dimension. Yet what's certain is that you have a part that you associate with.

Visual people are much more comfortable than kinesthetic or auditory people. Kinesthetic people are a little more concerned and less reflective, though.

We all have a tiny pinch of each of these inclinations. Perhaps the most important thing about NLP is it provides us with a fresh viewpoint on how we perceive reality, how we interpret things, and how we connect them to our personality.

Whether you are more relaxed, more anxious, more reflective, or more spontaneous, or you want to chat or are more attentive and introverted; this will all have an impact on how you see the world.

CHAPTER 22

THE ART OF ANALYZING BODY LANGUAGE

Body language is the subject of many studies and is the origin of many myths, such as one that says 93% of communication is non-verbal.

Many people who read it have become popular because they are devoted to repeating it, but the real research that started that belief presents too many flaws to take up.

But the impact of body language on our social skills is not negligible, in addition to being an excellent mirror of the real feelings of our interlocutors.

Certainly, you meet people who seem untrustworthy, especially if they are not unpleasant or unfriendly. You couldn't say what it was specifically, but they gave off an aura that didn't want to confess their true feelings.

That's because there is a discrepancy between their verbal communication and their body language.

On the other hand, other people give off a great charisma without any particular chat. Their physical expression is in harmony with their language and conveys confidence and warmth.

What is body language?

Body language is a form of communication that uses body and facial gestures, postures, and movements to convey information about the issuer's emotions and thoughts. Usually done at an unconscious level, it is often a very clear indicator of people's emotional state. Along with voice inflection, it is part of nonverbal communication.

The body language should not be regarded as absolute truth. There are many environmental factors that can affect the language of the body. That is why the conclusion of interpreting a single body symbol should never be reached. What is important is to observe each set of matching signs and eliminate possible external causes (temperature, noise, fatigue, etc.).

That said, let's look at everything we can communicate with the body and face.

Key to body language

1. The meaning of facial gestures

Since the face is a magnifier of emotion, it is said to be a reflection of the soul. However, as with nonverbal language interpretations, facial gestures are usually part of a global emotional state and can cause different interpretations. So be careful not to evaluate facial gestures individually.

152

Isn't it true that when a child sees what he dislikes, he covers his eyes so that it disappears from reality? Or doesn't he run to cover his mouth after he lies?

Now, for adults, the size is much smaller, but to some extent, we are still connected to this primitive behavior. And it gives a lot of clues. Because we can still detect in our face unconscious attempts to block what we say, hear and see.

In general, when someone puts their hand on their face, it is usually the product of negative thoughts such as anxiety and distrust. Here are some specific examples:

- **Covering or touching the mouth:** if done while speaking, it means trying to hide something. If it is done while listening, it may be a signal that the person believes something is hidden.
- **Touch the ear:** An unconscious expression of the desire to block audible words. If your listener does it while you are talking, it means he wants you to stop talking.
- **Touching the nose:** It may indicate that someone is lying. If you lie, catecholamines are released. Catecholamines can irritate the internal tissues of the nose and cause itching. It also happens when someone gets angry or worried.
- **Scratch one eye:** An attempt to block what you see so you don't have to face someone lying.

When talking to you, beware of people who frequently touch the nose and rub their eyes.

- **Scratch your neck:** A sign of uncertainty or doubt about what you are saying.
- **Bring your finger or something to your mouth**: it means anxiety, or you need to calm down with an unconscious expression of returning to the mother's safety.

2. Head position

Understanding the meaning of the various positions that the head can take is very effective in understanding one's true intentions such as likes, cooperation, and rog pride.

Pay special attention to a very exaggerated posture. Because they do it consciously to influence you.

- **Raise your head and project your chin forward**. This is a sign that aims to express positiveness and power clearly.
- **To nod:** it is a contagious obedience gesture that can convey positive feelings. It conveys interest and consent, but if it is done very quickly several times, it can tell you that they have already heard enough.
- **Tilt your head:** It is a sign of obedience by exposing your throat. Doing it while you're listening to someone's story increases your confidence in the talker. It has also been

observed for women to be used to show interest in men.

- **Support your face with your hands.** Usually, the face is exposed to "present" to the interlocutor. Therefore, it shows appeal to others.
- **Put the chin in hand:** If the palm is closed, it is an evaluation signal. If your palm is open, it can mean boredom or loss of interest.

3. It also talks about the appearance

Communication through the line of sight is largely related to the dilation or contraction of the pupil in response to the internal conditions we experience. That is why bright eyes are more attractive than dark eyes. Bright eyes can more clearly show pupil enlargement, a reaction associated with positive emotions.

When speaking, we usually maintain eye contact for 40-60% of the time. That's because your brain is busy trying to access the information (NLP assumes that depending on the type of information you are trying to get, you are looking sideways, but it has already been shown that this is not true).

In certain social situations, the lack of eye contact can be interpreted as tension or embarrassment. So the time required to access information without having to look away simply by pausing before responding can be obtained.

Looking directly at the eyes when you make a request can also help to increase persuasiveness. But there are other features of appearance:

- **Changing the size of the pupil:** Although it cannot be controlled, the presence of an enlarged pupil usually means that something comfortable is seen, but the constricted pupil is hostile. In any case, they are very subtle variations and are often hidden by environmental changes in light intensity. Mirroring neurons were also found to be responsible for students adjusting to the size of the interactor in an attempt to synchronize the body language to create a larger connection.

- **Raise your eyebrows:** A social greeting that means fear and lack of joy. Please don't do it in front of your favorite person.

- **Look up with your head down:** In the female sex, it is considered a posture that conveys the sensuality that attracts men. In fact, many of the women's profile pictures on online dating pages are taken from directly above (sometimes with the intention of showing the cleavage). In men, conversely, lower shots will appear higher and more dominant.

- **Maintain the appearance.** For women, establishing eye contact for 2-3 seconds before looking down is an indicator of sexual interest.

- **Flashing repeatedly:** Whether boredom or distrust, another way to try to block the vision of the person in front of you.
Looking sideways. This is another way to express boredom because you are unconsciously looking for an escape route.

4. Types of smiles

A smile is an endless source of meaning and emotion. There is an entire section about all the benefits of a smile and the possibility of communication with it. In addition, thanks to mirror neurons, smiles are very contagious acts that can cause very positive emotions in others.

However, not only one, but in practice, you can distinguish several types of smiles depending on the content of the communication.

- Fake smiles tend to be larger on the left side of the mouth because the most specific part of the brain that primarily controls the left side of the body is in the right hemisphere.
- A natural smile (or Duchenne smile) creates wrinkles next to the eyes, raises the cheeks, and slightly lowers the eyebrows.
- A tense smile with tight lips indicates that this person does not want to share feelings with you and is a clear sign of rejection.

The biological function of smiles is to create social bonds, support trust, and eliminate the sense of threat. It has also been proven to send submissions, that is why people who want to show their power and women who want to keep their authority in a typical male professional environment avoid smiles.

5. Arm position

The arm next to the hand supports most of the movements you perform. It can also protect the most vulnerable areas of your body in situations where you feel anxious.

Propriety taught us that the communication channel between the body and mind is reciprocal. When you experience emotions, your body reflects it unconsciously, and vice versa. When you take a spontaneous posture, your mind begins to experience the associated emotions. This is especially noticeable when arms are folded.

Many people think that they cross their arms because they feel more comfortable. However, gestures are seen naturally when they match the person's attitude. Science has already shown that although gestures seem comfortable, crossing them has an important approach. Do not cross your arms when playing with friends.

These are the things you say when you take a specific position with your hands.

- **Cross arms:** Shows misunderstanding and rejection. Avoid doing this unless you want to send this message to others. In a sensual context, women usually do this when they are in the presence of men who seem too aggressive or unattractive.

- **Crossing one hand in front to hold the other hand**: Means you are not confident in the need to feel in your arms.

- **Arms crossed with thumbs-up:** Defensive position, but at the same time want to express pride.

- **Joining hands in front of the genitals:** In men provides a sense of security in situations where there is sensitivity.

- **Putting your hands behind your back:** It shows confidence and fearlessness, revealing weaknesses such as the abdomen, throat, and perineum. Adopting this position in situations of uncertainty can be useful to try to gain confidence.

In general, crossing your arms means you are experiencing anxiety. Therefore, it is necessary to protect the body. There are many variations, such as adjusting the watch, placing the briefcase in front of the body, and holding the bag in front of the chest with both hands, all of which mean the same thing.

6. Hand gesture

Hands, along with arms, are one of the most mobile parts of the body, providing a vast record of nonverbal communication possibilities. The most common is to use them to indicate specific parts of the body to indicate authority or gender.

It also supports verbal messages and gives them great power.

- There is a part of the brain called the Broca region that is involved in the voice process. However, it has been proven to be activated by moving your hands. This means that the gesture is directly linked to the voice, so you can even improve your language skills by expressing yourself while doing so. Very useful for people who block when speaking in public!
- Research also shows that if you augment phrases with gestures, the words you use come to mind first, making your message more compelling and easier to understand. The survey found that the most persuasive gestures were in line with the meaning of words, such as going back to the past.

Below you will find everything known about the meaning of hand gestures.

- **Showing open palms:** Expresses honesty, and shows the opposite when closing the fist.

- **Hands in pockets:** Shows patriotism and lack of engagement in conversations and situations.
- **Emphasize something with your hand:** When you offer two views with your hand, what you like is usually reinforced with your dominant hand and palm up.
- **Intersect fingers of both hands**: Conveys a repressed, anxious, or negative attitude. If your interlocutor adopts this position, break it by giving him something so that he must hold it.
- **Integrated fingertips:** Expresses confidence and safety but can be confused with pride. It is very useful to detect if a rival has a good hand when playing poker.
- **Holding the other hand.** Because it is an attempt to control oneself, it is an attempt to express frustration or hide tension.
- **Show your thumb from your pocket.** Men represent attempts to show confidence and authority over women which attracts women, but in conflict situations, they can also be a way to communicate aggression.
- **Hide only your thumb in your pocket.** It is a posture that surrounds and emphasizes the genital area. Therefore, it is a sexually open attitude that men do to show women no fear or sexual interest.
- **Putting your hand on your waist.** Because one wants to increase physical presence, it shows a

slightly aggressive attitude. Many men use them to establish dominance in social circles and to look more masculine in the presence of those women that attract them. The more exposed the chest, the more active the sub-communication.

7. Leg position

The legs play a very interesting role in body language. Moving away from the central nervous system (brain), our rational minds can no longer control them and express greater freedom and inner feelings.

The further away your body is from your brain, the less control you have.

In general, people are programmed to get closer to what they want and get away from what they do not want. The way you place your feet indicates where you really want to go so that you can give the most valuable tips on nonverbal communication.

- **Advanced Feet:** The most advanced foot is almost always where you want to go. In a social situation with several people, you point to the most interesting and attractive person. If you want someone to feel attentive and emotional, make sure your feet are pointing toward him. Similarly, when the caller points to the door and not to you, it is a clear sign that they want to end the conversation.

- **Crossed legs:** A defensive and closed posture that protects the genitals. In the context of courtship, women can convey the sexual rejection of men. In social situations, sitting with arms and legs crossed probably means leaving the conversation. In fact, researchers Alain and Barbara Pairs conducted experiments that show that when they hear a meeting with crossed arms and legs, they don't remember the details of the meeting.

- **Sit with one foot up to the other:** Usually, a man who is competitive and ready to discuss. That would be the display version of the sitting crotch.

- **Very separate legs:** A basically masculine gesture that wants to convey dominance and territoriality.

- **Sit with curled feet:** In women, it usually means some shyness and introversion.

- **Sitting one leg side by side on the other:** This position is more squeezed and provides a younger and more sensual appearance. So if you try to pay attention to your legs, it can be interpreted as courtship by a woman.

Learning to detect language and body language discrepancies is very helpful. Since humans cannot control all the signals they emit, what the body shows is usually very reliable.

THE 5 PRACTICAL KEYS TO MASTERING NONVERBAL LANGUAGE

Not only words are important to communicate and relate, but non-verbal language is decisive in most situations, in what we say and how we say it. It is the perfect accompaniment to words. It is therefore important to learn to dominate non-verbal language so as to remove the mask from words, consequently to people.

How to dominate non-verbal language

Know yourself

A key tip for mastering non-verbal language is to know yourself. It's the best way to get information about yourself, to know who you really are.

That is to say, if we focus well, we can observe how we really are. What does it mean when you touch an eye? Think about what is happening at that moment in your mind and so you will know why you expressed that typical act of non-verbal language.

It may seem like a simple exercise, but it is absolutely not the case. It will become very useful in every area of your life, because the more one knows, the greater chance one will have of transforming one's existence into what one really wants.

"People often say they haven't found themselves yet. But the self is not something that is found but that is created. "

-Thomas Szasz-

The face reflects the soul

They say that the face is the mirror of the soul, its true reflection. There are certainly people capable of dominating non-verbal language so as not to show others what is going on in their minds and their right mood. In general, however, we can learn a lot about them through their faces and expressions.

The face has a vast number of facial muscles, with extraordinary functions. They show our right mood. There is even science that bases its theories on facial features; it's called morpho psychology. It is therefore clear that thanks to his face, you can know a lot about a person.

How can you practice such facial gestures to dominate non-verbal language and avoid the externalization of emotions? This is a challenging practice. The face and its musculature were created to show elemental emotions such as anger, sadness, surprise, or joy. Each of them involves several mechanisms. Mastering them is a difficult task.

In this sense, when you dominate a non-verbal language, the only thing you can do to avoid showing emotions is to fake them. It would be like hiding real feelings.

It would be good to look at yourself in the mirror for a long time until you manage to dominate your statements. For example, if you feel joy, put on your sad face, exercising with the muscles that are activated when you display any emotions until you can control them.

Look in the eyes

A good technique to master non-verbal language is to look directly into the eyes. We must not forget that constantly avoiding the eyes of others shows terrible insecurity and lack of self-confidence.

Looking directly into the eyes of the interlocutor, on the other hand, gives the feeling of participating in a conversation between peers, showing less of themselves. It is an important piece to dominate non-verbal language since in this way you externalize what you really want to show to the other person.

Be natural

To dominate non-verbal language, nothing works like behaving in a natural way, being yourself. The more you know each other, the less you will worry about showing something undesirable. In this sense, it will become easier to establish relationships with other people and you will have no worries about what you will show or not through your gestures.

Learn to be yourself, to emphasize the movements that are proper to your person, avoiding the mannerisms and elements that do not belong to your true nature. Those acquired vices are easily interpreted by others.

Keep calm

To appear relaxed, in full calm, is a simple form of dominating non-verbal language. Anxiety, nerves or anger lead us to externalize our way of being too much through gestures and THE face.

"A man who finds no satisfaction in himself will seek it in vain elsewhere."

-La Rochefoucauld-

BODY LANGUAGE AND EMOTIONS

No matter how much you try to keep a neutral expression when you don't want to reveal your emotions to others, you may not even realize how important it is to control your body language when you want to appear unfathomable. You may be dating a person you met on a dating app and now want to meet in person. And as you sit and wait for that very important first encounter, you retain the face shape that you feel is neutral. Unfortunately, you didn't pay attention to do the same thing with your body. You kick your legs, rollover, and your hands are restless. Your potential partner will now be able to recognize that you are tense and nervous, and the rest of the evening will not go the way you planned. According to a recent study by Gijsbert Bijlstra and colleagues (2018) from Radboud University in the Netherlands, under certain conditions, people recognize emotions better through body language than through facial expressions.

However, you will rarely find yourself in a situation where you read someone's emotions from a completely neutral standpoint, and your expectations do not play a role in interpreting that person's body language.

Bijlstra and colleagues have suggested that the process of reading the speech of other people's bodies is influenced by signs of the so-called "social category" that determine one's position in society. In their study, they note that gender cannot be separated from how others perceive you and interpret your emotional expression. If you are a man and exhibit a "typical" male emotion, such as anger, others will notice it faster than displaying the same emotion if you are a woman. Conversely, if you are a woman and exhibit a typical feminine emotion, such as sadness, people will notice it faster than if it is shown by a man.

To test the claim that gender influences the perception of body language, Dutch authors created silhouettes of men and women who display the same emotions. Their experiment participants performed a task of classifying the speed at which they needed to identify those emotions as quickly as possible. As predicted, trial participants identified anger in men and sadness in women more quickly than anger in women and sadness in men.

This research shows that expectations truly influence the way we identify emotions in the form of stereotypes about the social categorization they belong to. Admittedly, gender was the only social cue investigated. It would be perfectly reasonable to expect other categories such as age, race, and social status to be able to play similar roles that influence how we see other people.

Or, if we turn this around, research also implies that the way others perceive you is influenced by the social characteristics you submit to the social categories you represent. If an observer is programmed to see only a man as angry and a woman as sad, it means that without deliberately presenting yourself as an angry or sad person, your gender can lead people to interpret your body language in a stereotypical manner. Therefore, it can be quite difficult for women not to turn sad and for men not to turn angry.

Lastly, body language is a form of communication that can both help and unwind your relationship. Put it to your advantage by recognizing prejudices that prevent the connection from working properly.

HOW TO READ BODY LANGUAGE FAST

Knowing how to interpret another person's body language requires a closer relationship because non-verbal communication accounts for up to 60% of all interpersonal communication. Therefore, paying attention to the signals sent through body language and interpreting them successfully is a very useful skill. With a little care, you can learn to decipher these cues correctly and practice hard to make this habit instinct.

1. Interpreting emotional signs

Be careful not to cry because we believe that most cultures are triggered by emotional explosions. Tears are often seen as a sign of suffering and sorrow. They are not only manifested through laughter and humor but are also expressions of happiness. Therefore, you need to look at other signs to determine the proper context for tears.

- A person may force or manipulate a cry to gain empathy or to deceive others. This practice is known as "crocodile tears." An informal expression based on the myth of "crying" when a crocodile catches prey.

Watch for signs of anger and threats. Threat signs include a V-shaped eyebrow, wide eyes, open mouth, or lower lip corners.

- A tightly crossed arm is a common sign of irritation and rejection.

Watch for signs of anxiety. When anxiety occurs, people blink more, face movement increases, and lips stretch to form thin lines.

- Anxious people lose their composure and can move their hands over and over without stopping.
- Another way to show anxiety is to step and move your feet unconsciously.

Note the embarrassing expression. We smile and show embarrassment in a controlled or tense manner, looking away or turning the head sideways.

- If you look too much at the floor, you are very likely to be shy or embarrassed. You look down when you're upset or want to hide your emotions. When people spend a lot of time looking at the floor, they usually think bad things and experience uncomfortable feelings.

Observe the expression of pride. Individuals show pride by carefully smiling, tilting their heads back and placing their hands on their hips.

2. Interpretation of interpersonal signs

Assess distance and proximity: These are ways to

communicate the status of interpersonal relationships. Touch and physical proximity show love and affection.

- Two people in an intimate relationship require less personal space than two strangers.
- It is important to note that personal spaces are culturally fluid. So, keep in mind that what is considered nearby in one country may be considered far in another.

Please read people's eyes. According to research, if an individual has an interesting conversation, they may see the recipient's face for about 80% of the time. However, the focus is not only on the eyes. The line of sight sometimes moves to the lips and nose and may face downward, but is always placed on the other person's eyes.

- Usually, when someone looks up to the right during a conversation, they are bored and not interested in speaking.
- Inflated students are interested in what is happening. However, be aware that many substances can cause this expansion, such as alcohol, cocaine, amphetamine, and LSD.
- Eye contact is also widely used to show integrity. Too much or aggressiveness with someone's eyes suggests that you are very aware of the message you want to convey. Therefore, if an individual does not want to lie and appear to avoid the

interlocutor, he can intentionally change the way he maintains eye contact. This is a famous sign of a lie. However, as I said, take into account the various individual differences in associating eye contact with lies.

Observe the posture. The person who puts his arm behind his neck or head gives a message that he is speaking or perhaps that he is generally a relaxed individual.

- The tight crossing of arms and legs often indicates resistance and poor acceptability. In general, when we adopt this stance, we inform others that we are mentally, emotionally and physically closed.
- In a study where 2,000 transactions were recorded on videotape to assess the negotiator's body language, no transaction was made with either of the participants' arms or legs crossed.

3. Interpretation of signs of attraction

Analyze eye contact. Watching someone's eyes is a sign of attraction because it flashes 6 to 10 times a minute than the normal average.

- Keep in mind that flashing is a flickering or attractive sign, but this is not true for all cultures. Some Asians are frustrated with the wink and consider it rude.

173

Pay attention to certain facial expressions. Since smiles are one of the clearest signs of attraction, you will learn to decipher forced smiles from real smiles. We know that a smile is false when it doesn't move the corners of the eyes. True smiles often cause wrinkles in the corners of the eyes. Wrinkles do not appear when people laugh.

- Raising the eyebrows is another sign related to flirting.

Consider the person's gesture and posture. In general, individuals tend to approach the people they are attracted to. They may lean towards you or may be more direct and touch you. Lightly touching or stroking someone's arm is a sign of attraction.

- They are also interested in turning their feet forward attracted people.
- An upward-facing palm suggests acceptability and is another indicator of love interest.

Don't forget the gender difference. Men and women can show physical attraction in a variety of ways.

- Men lean forward and can turn their torso towards those who they are interested in. Meanwhile, a woman who meets his intentions pulls his torso apart and leans back.
- A man in love with someone can raise his hand over his head at a 90-degree angle.

- When a woman expresses her charm, she can touch her body with her hand in the area between her waist and chin, with her arms open.

4. Interpreting power signals

Pay attention to eye contact. If you look at it, the movement communication channel is the main way to convey control. Those who want to prove authority have the freedom to face and evaluate others while maintaining direct eye contact. They will also be the last people to suspend eye contact.

- If you want to exercise power, keep in mind that constant eye contact can intimidate others.

Evaluate facial expressions. If you think seriously, those who want to show an advantage can avoid smiles and squeeze their lips.

Analyze gestures and postures. Gestures can show superiority. Pointing at others and making many gestures is a way to show power. One also shows superiority when he is relaxed but at the same time maintains a higher posture than others and occupies more body space.

- The dominant individual also has a very firm handshake. To show control, they often hang up with their hands up and greet with a firm and lasting grip.

Consider how someone controls your space. A high person generally maintains a larger physical space when interacting with a lower person. Authoritarians often occupy more space to express the rule of the situation. In other words, a vast attitude shows success and power.

- It also works when you decide to stand instead of sit. Standing up (especially in front of everyone) is considered a posture of power.
- Furthermore, rather than bend forward, you can increase your confidence by keeping your back straight and keeping your shoulders back. A sloppy posture that leans forward conveys anxiety.
- The dominant individual also guides the rest of the group, walking in front of everyone and first through the door. They like to be in front.

Notice how and when people touch other people. Those who show superiority are so confident that they easily touch other people. In general, in situations where one person has more authority than another, the most powerful individuals tend to touch the lower position person more often.

- In social situations where both parties are in the same position, people respond to the ring in a similar manner.

5. Understanding body language

Note that the interpretation of body language is a complex task. Nonverbal behavior is complex. Because we are all different and appear in the world in various ways. Reading body language can be difficult because it requires a general context to be able to interpret the received signal. For example, was this person fighting with his wife or saying he could not be promoted? Was she visibly anxious at lunch?

- Whenever possible, when interpreting someone's body language, you need to consider their personality and language behavior, social factors, and the surrounding environment. Such information is not always available but can be very helpful in reading body language. Because people are complex, communicating in complex ways through the body is natural!
- Compare the habits of reading body language and watching your favorite TV show. In addition to watching program scenes, you can understand the meaning of the problem scene correctly and understand the entire episode. You are also very likely to remember past episodes, character stories, and the entire plot. When interpreting body language, you should also pay attention to the overall context!

Remember that nonverbal communication varies from culture to culture. Some emotions and expressions in body language have culturally specific meanings.

- People with certain conditions such as the autism spectrum may behave differently, such as not being able to see the recipient while listening.
- For example, in Finnish culture, people are receptive to seeing their eyes. On the other hand, eye contact is considered to be a sign of Japanese anger.
- Another example: In Western cultures, when you are comfortable, they lean on you and leave their face and body facing you.
- Keep in mind that although specific expressions of emotion vary from culture to culture, some studies have shown that specific expressions of body language are universal. This is especially true for domination and submission communication. For example, in many different cultures, maintaining a curved posture indicates obedience.

Note that the interpretation depends on the communication channel. In non-language channels, messages or signals are sent without words. The most important non-verbal channels include movement forms (eye contact, facial expression, body language), tactile (touch), and proxyomic (personal space) communication. That is, the media determines the message.

- As a rule, it is easy to interpret facial expressions, followed by body language, followed by touch and personal space.
- There are several variations within each channel. For example, not all facial expressions are equally easy to understand, but there is a tendency to read comfortable facial expressions rather than unpleasant facial expressions. One study shows that people can better interpret signs of happiness, joy, and excitement compared to anger, sadness, fear, and disgust.

CHAPTER 23

OPTIMISTIC AND PESSIMISTIC PEOPLE

Optimism or pessimism are best understood from the comparison of the attitudes of each point of view. The same person can go through moments of optimism and others of greater pessimism in their own life. However, when each human being looks with sincerity inside, he can also realize what is the most common tendency in his life or in his presence. What are the characteristics of optimistic and pessimistic people?

How does an optimistic person act?

Optimism produces admiration since most people want to live it in practice. However, optimism is not innate but is cultivated through habits marked by constancy. How does an optimistic person act?

1. Sense of humor

They are people who have the ability to relativize external difficulties and circumstances through a funny look that puts the spotlight on some comic aspect of reality itself. The sense of humor is a personal decision since each person can cultivate it individually.

2. *Observe things in context*

In relation to the previous point, optimistic people are also able to relativize certain circumstances because they attend to the context of what happened and observe that everything happens, and nothing remains. That is to say, what today is fully topical, in just a few days will be passed. Therefore, optimists live the present with a constructive vision.

3. *Authenticity*

True optimism is only effective when it is sincere. From this perspective, one of the characteristics of optimistic people is that they radiate light where they are because they spread their good energy to others through reflections, words, and attitudes.

4. *Realistic*

Sometimes those who live a moment of pessimism feel that optimists move away from reality in their interpretations. However, truly effective positive thinking is one that also integrates the reality of life. Optimistic people also experience difficulties and difficult times. However, they try to focus on dealing with what they can manage instead of worrying chronically. They try to generate alternatives; they look for help if they need it and they don't lock themselves up.

5. Emotional well-being

Much of the well-being that optimistic people experience depends on their own attitude. That is, this sense of harmony is a reflection of the positive impact that happy thoughts produce on the emotional level through a friendly and constructive inner dialogue. The optimist has a constructive self-image of himself and the way in which he observes influences the way he positions himself in the different spheres of his life.

What does it mean to be a pessimistic person?

Optimistic people also have moments of pessimism. And those who feel more pessimistic have moments of optimism. For this reason, both concepts feedback on the experience of living itself. The main difference between optimism and pessimism may be the way of approaching life and the challenges that it proposes. What are the characteristics of people who tend to think negatively?

1. The negative view of reality

This can be observed in all-time fragments. For example, the protagonist remembers more frequently the sad situations of yesterday or lives with the perception of chronic longing that prevents him from enjoying the present. In the same way, he focuses more on the shortcomings than on the reasons for gratitude for the

182

present. Similarly, he visualizes the future from the prism of insecurity. Therefore, pessimism, like optimism, shows a look at reality.

2. Frequent complaints

If in the plane of thought there are limiting beliefs that boycott the potential of that person, in the plane of verbal expression the tendency to complain arises as a response of personal dissatisfaction. The complaint does not solve anything by itself, however, it seems a mantra for those who contemplate reality from the perspective of self-pity, the feeling of bad luck, comparison with others or fear. Sometimes, pessimistic people conclude that they have no luck because this is the message that they have repeated to themselves on countless occasions.

3. They have a wrong picture of themselves

Pessimistic people have a distorted view of their abilities and talent. And often they confuse the way they see themselves with the way they think they are seen by others. For example, they don't feel comfortable when they receive words of recognition because they don't think they really deserve it. Pessimism is one of the characteristics of people with low self-esteem.

4. They are compared with others

Pessimistic people can lose doses of energy in the

recurring tendency to live from comparison by idealizing others and placing themselves in the role of inferiority.

5. Insecurity

There are so many negative thoughts that can go through the mind of a person throughout a single day that these beliefs are transferred to the plane of action in the form of an attitude marked by insecurity in new situations that produce fear.

How to become an optimistic person

Optimism and pessimism are not absolute concepts since every human being has both negative and happy thoughts. The characteristics of optimistic and pessimistic people can appear in the same individual simultaneously. So, the question is, "Is it better to be optimistic or pessimistic?" Sometimes, it may not make much sense.

How to have an optimistic attitude

However, if a person feels that the weight of negativity considerably exceeds the good energy of optimism, then he can commit to his own ability to initiate a process of personal change. Because optimism is not an exclusive privilege of those who feel this way, but a possible and attainable goal. How to become an optimistic person?

- Just as there is no definitive limit on wisdom, there is no maximum limit on optimism. Therefore, try to value those simple day-to-day actions that you exercise in order to take care of yourself.

- Decide to be optimistic. To do this, make a list of reasons why you want to achieve this mission. These reasons constitute an important source of your motivation. When you face a complex situation, remember that you are free to decide how you want to respond to it. Which option compensates you the most? Choose the one that suits you best.

- Personal growth courses. As important as professional training is, so is life training. Self-knowledge workshops can mark a turning point in those who run new resources and resilience skills in the context of training sessions guided by experts in psychology.

- Bring humor to your life through cinema, theater, monologues, literature and conversations with friends. The stimulation of humor sharpens your ingenuity for the benefit of happiness.

If you want to change your life, start by changing your attitude.

CHAPTER 24

HOW TO INCREASE SELF-ESTEEM WITH BODY LANGUAGE

Although we do not say a word, body language reveals what we feel inside ourselves. Low self-esteem is reflected in body language. Your body is influenced by your thoughts and vice versa. One way to improve your self-esteem is by modifying your body language.

Body language and self-esteem

Your body language, which is simply what you transmit through your body movements and postures, can sabotage what you are saying.

For example: If you say that you know how to do something very well and at the same time your hands perspire and you do not make eye contact, what you are really transmitting with your body is that you feel insecure about yourself.

Therefore, this will be an inconsistency between what he says and how he moves.

Body language of people with high self-esteem

People with high self-esteem have the following traits:

- Head up
- Right-back
- Movements are calm and safe

One way to improve your self-esteem is by modifying your body language as follows:

- Always sit with your back straight.
- Put a smile on your face.
- Make direct contact with the eyes of the person in front of you.
- Keep your body relaxed, avoid crossing, and uncrossing your legs.
- Avoid fiddling with something in your hands to avoid gestures that show nervousness.
- Always keep your eyes forward, showing self-confidence.

Remember that people with high self-esteem and self-confidence are not unhappy, bored, or without a lack of interest because they feel comfortable with themselves.

Keep in mind that when we are in front of a stranger, body language is the first thing they see. We can, therefore, increase our self-esteem and self-confidence, if when we feel insecure, we turn our backs, raise our heads, and breathe slowly and deeply.

Changing your posture will cause you to feel internal to change, as well. The more you practice this, the more natural it will become for you.

CHAPTER 25

HOW TO CHANGE YOUR EMOTIONS WITH YOUR BODY

We all know that unpleasant emotions can trigger bodily reactions such as headaches, indigestion, or rashes, but also, imbalances in body systems can badly affect mood. Ancient treatment systems say that if we excrete too much stomach acid, which happens because of a disorderly diet, we may suffer from depression or explosive mood swings. Learn to get your body back in balance.

King David was said that a cheerful heart is an excellent remedy and that a cheerful spirit dries the bones. These words beautifully summarize the wisdom of many ancient healing systems like Ayurveda, Siddha medicine, and traditional Chinese medicine. All ancient civilizations have long woven the knowledge that mind, body, and spirit are connected, and that a long and happy life requires their harmony. They act on each other in a constant game of energy.

Chemical messages

Emotions and thoughts are forms of energy that, like electricity, flow through our bodies. Every emotion and thought has a different frequency that triggers the release of certain neuropeptides and hormones. Neuropeptides are chemical substances that carry chemical "messages" (emotions and thoughts) between the nerve cells of our body, creating a physiological response. Our body produces hundreds of different neuropeptides, each of which governs some other physiological functions.

Thus, for example, happiness, pleasure, and laughter stimulate the release of endorphins, the "happiness hormone," which reduces pain and reduces anxiety and tension, relaxes muscles, and strengthens our immune system. So, it helps us feel good. Otherwise, while we are scared, anxious, or stressed, for example, hormones such as adrenaline, noradrenaline, and cortisol are secreted. They, in turn, cause rapid heartbeat, rapid shallow breathing, slight sweating, and muscle tension.

In extremely stressful situations or when stress lasts too long, gastric acid secretion increases. Such excessive and too long excretion of acid interferes with the functioning of all systems in the body. Namely, these changes on the physical plane, which throw us off balance, affect the invisible part of us—our emotions, psyche, and the amount of vital energy that we have.

Tired and needless

According to naturopathy or natural medicine, if there is no complete emptying of the intestines, many bacteria begin to multiply on the matter that builds up in them over time.

They create toxic gases that then pass through the intestinal walls into the bloodstream and flow throughout the body. This means that each cell and tissue is soaked in toxic blood, making their detoxification process even more difficult. When such blood reaches the brain, we may begin to feel tired and unwell, with frequent periods of lethargy and even depression.

Traditional healing systems recognize that gastric acid vapor can cause sinus and skin problems, but there may be some mental health problems. Naturopaths believe that elevated levels of gastric acid can affect the brain and manifest in sudden mood swings—often in the form of outbursts of hatred, jealousy and anger.

As a proven solution for such moods, naturopaths recommend several days of juice therapy—when meals should be replaced with fresh fruit and vegetable juices. Following such fasting, you should adjust your diet, exclude fried foods, increase your intake of fresh, fiber-rich raw foods, and increase your intake of water.

Emotions and immunity

More recently, too, science recognizes that through thoughts and emotions, we can manage the body and overall health. This deals with psychoneuroimmunology, a branch of science that studies the connection between emotions and the functioning of the immune, nervous, and endocrine systems. It could be said that thoughts and emotions are the first steps towards physical reactions. Every time we think of something, it triggers a certain emotion that triggers a certain physical reaction.

Thus, for example, our anger causes our muscles to tighten, and blood pressure rises; sadness causes tears that can relax us; happiness produces a laugh that can energize us... Equally, when we are scared or nervous, our mouths dry and our palms sweat. But as we change our minds, so will our physical reactions to them, according to the Ayurvedic sages who have always emphasized that the mind controls the body. The mind is responsible for perception, thinking, understanding, and decision making.

Negative thinking, therefore, weakens Ojas (strength), Tejas (inner radiance) and prana (vital energy), and on the physical level, the immune system, spleen, and other vital organs. Also, this millennial knowledge views negative emotions as emotional toxins. Failure to remove them from the body within a given time may cause the development of mental disorders, such as neurosis or depression. If we continue to ignore these conditions, it is easily possible that they will develop into more severe mental disorders.

CONCLUSION

People seeking to exercise dominance or control over others often make rapid and imprecise movements with their hands. It is common for them to do what we commonly know as "flipping." That is, moving your hands up and down to give more emphasis to what they are saying. Also, to show more energy and forcefulness.

Another frequent gesture in the body language of controlling people is the index finger pointing towards the other. This is a gesture that, in principle, is a warning sign. However, it is also implicitly an indication and even an accusation. This, of course, conditions the emotional state of who is singled out. It gives control to whoever wields it and takes it away from his interlocutor.

On the other hand, dominant people often use their arms to increase the space they occupy. They put their hands on the waist in an attitude of protest or cross their arms. If they are standing and the other is sitting, it is also common for them to close their fists and rest them on the table.

All of these elements of the body language of controlling people can also be used in their favor. According to experts on the subject, adopting these gestures and postures, at times when we feel intimidated or vulnerable, helps us regain a sense of control.

DARK PSYCHOLOGY

Learn How to Strategically Plant Yourself in Anyone's Mind without Arousing Suspicion

Henry Wood

INTRODUCTION

The term 'Dark Psychology' refers to a group of three personality traits: narcissism, Machiavellianism, and psychopathy. All three characters are associated with an insensitive-manipulative relationship style.

Factor analysis shows that among the Big Five, poor tolerance correlates most strongly with Dark Psychology, while neuroticism's lack of conscientiousness is associated with Machiavellianism and psychopathy.

The use of the word "dark" implies that people who score high on these traits have malicious qualities.

Narcissism is characterized by pride, self-centeredness, grandiosity, and a lack of empathy.

Machiavellianism is characterized by the tendency to exploit and manipulate others, a disregard for moral ideas, and a focus on self-interest and deception.

Psychopathy is characterized by anti-social behavior, selfishness, numbness, impulsiveness, and mercilessness.

According to studies, some women were attracted to men with psychopathic, Machiavellian or narcissistic features, and others were not. Their characteristics ranged from 'aggressive' and 'less cheerful' to psychopathic tendencies, 'dishonest' for Machiavellian, and 'masculine' and 'dominant' for narcissistic.

The scientists checked whether women with preferences for the personality traits of the dark triad in the faces of men were related to reproductive success. Previous studies had found that of the three dark triad features, narcissism was linked to physical and mental health in men as well as social progress.

"We were able to show that women's preference for narcissism was most linked to their reproductive success, and we found that women with a preference for 'narcissistic' faces had had more children."

Women with a clear preference for Machiavellian male faces registered less offspring with little interest in this trait than participants of the same generation.

For women with a preference for men with 'psychopathic' faces, there was no relation to the current number of offspring.

Psychologists call the combination of narcissism, Machiavellianism, and psychopathy the "dark triad." Anyone who embodies them gets through life very well, mainly because nobody stops them.

Psychopathy is the darkest of the three facets. Those who achieve high values here are cold-hearted, impulsive, and fearless. This makes the psychopath particularly risk conscious. He is not afraid of consequences, and remorse is foreign to him.

What the three characteristics have in common is their low social tolerance, which is shown by ruthlessness and a tendency to deceive others, as well as an unwillingness to abide by rules or moral principles.

CHAPTER 1

WHAT'S DARK PSYCHOLOGY?

The personality of a person is so complex that you can never grasp it 100 percent, neither with other people nor with yourself. Some traits are innate, others acquired in education, and still, others have developed or have been lost in the course of life. Man is in a constant change, and his personality is not set in stone. Nevertheless, there are fundamental personality traits in every person, which shape their character in their unique constellation and only change in the rarest of cases—for example, through strokes of fate or long-term therapy:

A helpful and empathic person does not suddenly become emotionally cold and a manipulative exploiter.

A narcissist does not suddenly develop healthy self-confidence and a high degree of empathy for his social environment.

A self-actor does not suddenly wake up one morning as a humble and shy person.

People can slip into different roles or work on themselves in terms of personality development. But such fundamental personality traits cannot be changed—at least not easily, not quickly and often not without external help. It is, therefore, exhilarating to go into self-reflection and to explore your personality traits. At the latest, when you next sit in front of your application documents or prepare for an interview, you will be forced to do so anyway. It is not without reason that almost all HR managers finally ask about your strengths and weaknesses.

The relationship between your personality and career

The dark personality traits are not small weaknesses like "I just can't resist chocolate," but are eleven of the essential and hardly changeable personality traits that have adverse effects—especially in professional life. A study found that a strong manifestation of one of these weaknesses or a corresponding combination of the eleven dark personality traits always became a hindrance to careers over time, regardless of how successful they were at the beginning. This means that you can be successful despite these dark personality traits, but never in the long run.

On the other hand, you must not have certain dark personality traits or weaknesses. But if you do, you should work quickly to get rid of them or at least to soften them. Your personality is, therefore, the fundamental factor that decides whether you succeed or fail in your professional life. Accordingly, you should not only focus on your strengths in your personal development but also work on your weaknesses.

What are the eleven dark personality traits?

In their study, Joyce and Robert Hogan exposed 11 personality traits that are incredibly harmful to your career. Take an honest look at the descriptions below and ask yourself whether you can find these weaknesses. But please do not be alarmed: everyone will find themselves in one or more of these dark personality traits. As already mentioned, the human personality is extremely complex. This does not mean that you are doomed to failure. This is only the case if there is a correspondingly strong expression or if these personality traits are combined in a toxic way. So, if you notice a weak expression in yourself, it is completely normal.

1. Wicked

While many of the other dark personality traits may sound neutral or even positive at first glance, the case with the malicious character type is clear. They are risk-taking people who like to test their limits and those of their social environment and are always looking for the next "kick." They are ruthless and not very empathetic. The malicious personality trait is particularly pronounced in disorders such as narcissism or psychopathy.

Wicked people love the risk and can often appear charming and extremely convincing, for example, due to narcissistic features. As a result, they quickly climb the career ladder and are incredibly successful at the start of their careers.

Only with time does their impulsive and manipulative nature put a spanner in the works. They get more and more into interpersonal conflicts, get caught up in a lie, or take too significant a risk and fail.

2. Resourceful

While a tangible disorder often accompanies a malicious personality trait, its career damage is apparent. But what about the other ten? At first glance, ingenuity sounds anything but bad. It is the ability to think creatively and "differently" than maybe your colleagues or superiors. As visionaries, people who have this dark personality trait are predestined for independence.

In the long run, however, the personality trait makes one too jumpy to work consistently on a goal or in a job. Sometimes the ideas get so crazy that they are interesting but merely unrealistic. As important as visionaries are for a company, they are mostly not suitable as managers. In the wrong environment without appropriate support, the career of these people comes to a halt sooner or later.

3. Excitable

People with a robust, sensitive personality trait are less choleric than constantly dissatisfied whining. They get excited quickly and then float in the highest spheres of happiness, but unfortunately, this condition never lasts long. Instead, they move in constant discontent most of the time. This is going through, for example:

- Mood swings
- Emotional instability
- Too high demands

They are difficult to please and quickly get on the nerves of their professional environment. When excitable people are in their enthusiastic phase, they can sweep away, inspire, and motivate those around them. These would be the perfect qualities for a manager. Unfortunately, their volatility knows how to prevent this hierarchical rise as well as their regular outbursts of anger or nagging, which increasingly cause interpersonal conflicts.

4. Colorful

The colorful personality type is, of course, to be understood metaphorically. A "colorful" trait describes a very striking personality. She is extravagant, likes to be the center of attention, and therefore always attracts attention. Unfortunately, she is accordingly self-centered and tends to drama always. Thus, "colorful" employees in the company are welcome entertainers to loosen up the dreary day-to-day work or to bring a little zest to the team, but their social skills are not sufficient for a steep career. Because of their self-centeredness, they tend to interrupt their counterparts and act with little empathy.

5. Obedient

People with the obedient personality trait avoid any conflict and would, therefore, do everything to please their counterpart—for example, the manager. They are dutiful, disciplined, and in need of harmony. Their loyalty and diligence make these people the "perfect" employees. Unfortunately, because of their fear of mistakes, they are unable to act and work independently. They cannot deal with conflicts that are unfortunately unavoidable in companies, and their submissive nature makes them unsuitable for management.

6. Leisurely

The leisurely personality type is described in English as "Leisurely," which refers to the term "leisure time." It is a personality trait that presents itself cooperatively and socially in professional life but places more value on leisure time than the job. As soon as work and private life get in the way, people with a pronounced leisurely personality tend to be stubborn and irritable.

7. Conscientious

The conscientious person works meticulously. He quickly gets lost in detail and thereby loses a lot of valuable working time. People with an unusually careful personality trait, therefore, tend to perfection and stand in the way of their careers themselves. While they are great for high-responsibility jobs because they make very few mistakes, they would simply be too unproductive in a leadership position.

8. Suspicious

People who have very questionable traits have usually experienced many disappointments in life. They try to protect themselves from further injuries through cynicism and low expectations. They are fundamentally skeptical, sensitive to any criticism which they perceive as a personal injury and have a cynical worldview—especially towards other people.

These "cynics" always expect the worst and assume that their social environment is hostile to them. Suspicious people often have a high level of empathy and sensitivity. They have a feeling for falsehoods, manipulations, or situations in which something is "lazy." They are, therefore, ideally suited for a position with a high level of responsibility, perhaps even the foundation of your own company. Unfortunately, they appear to be quarrelsome, exhausting, or simply unappealing on their social environment. And since relationships are the be-all and end-all for professional success, too much distrust is out of place here.

9. Daring

The daring personality trait means that those affected have exaggerated self-esteem and are overly self-confident, even arrogant. On the one hand, as unappealing as it may sound, it is a career-enhancing characteristic.

However, the "daring" employee likes to take it to the extreme. He appears determined, almost know-it-all, and thereby offends his counterpart in the head. At some point, due to his seemingly unshakable self-confidence and self-portrayal, he gets on his nerves and, therefore, on the decision-makers in the company. The steep career often works at the beginning, but as soon as the big promises turn out to be empty, the hierarchical ascent usually ends suddenly.

10. Reluctant

The reserved personality trait stands in complete contrast to the daring personality. Nevertheless, this is at least as harmful to your career. Resistant characters appear shy, not natural to make decisions, and exaggeratedly cautious. It takes a long time to accept changes and adapt to them. Taking risks would be just as unthinkable for such people as making quick and flexible decisions. In the complex business world, this is an absolute poison for your career. Nevertheless, people with these personality traits can be successful in a suitable position due to their care and restraint—just not as a manager.

11. Doubtful

The dubious personality trait is closely related to the reserved one. He achieves a high degree of detachment and reserve. This has an unapproachable effect on the social environment, to the point of being arrogant or utterly "strange." In any case, people with a pronounced doubtful personality trait are complicated to assess for their counterparts. They are indifferent to the feelings of their social environment and thus appear emotionally cold. With the dubious personality type, his stoic calm, especially in stressful situations, can be a plus for his career. He gives orientation to his employees or team members and always keeps a cool head.

However, his lack of social skills will sooner or later put a spanner in the works because they are essential for a management position.

A little more sensitivity and empathy would be necessary with the doubtful personality trait to be permanently successful in the job.

Are the dark personality traits "curable"?

Given this, wouldn't it be desirable if such dark personality traits could be cured? For sure! Unfortunately, this is only possible—if at all—by the person concerned. However, some personality traits such as the daring personality stand in the way of healing. After all, it is almost impossible for people with a bold personality to go into self-criticism and realize that they need to be improved at this point. This would ultimately contradict their overconfidence. On the other hand, if you are capable of self-reflection and perceive dark personality traits, you can certainly work on them.

All in all, changing the basic personality traits is not always possible, and if so, only with a high degree of self-reflection and self-discipline. In addition, you always need time for personal development. If, on the other hand, you are already able to find yourself in one of the dark traits mentioned, you have taken an important first step in the right direction. We can only congratulate you on this. So, it is not impossible to become a permanently successful person despite a "dark personality." Unfortunately, it is not easy either.

Two ways to discover your dark side

How to make the invisible visible?

Discovering your dark side is not an easy task, mainly because the "dark side" is that part of us that, many times, we still have not accepted.

The shadow

As a child, you receive a significant amount of judgments about what is right and what is wrong about you, your behavior, or your feelings. So at a very young age, you already have a clear understanding of what is appreciated and valued by your parents, and whatnot.

For example, if your parents criticize you for crying, you

learn that showing strength is recognized and accepted, but showing weakness is not. Every time you feel weak, you will give up that feeling and send it to the subconscious or shadow.

Thus, it will be created as a "bag" in which each behavior that is criticized, each thought that is despised or each emotion that is not valued, will be sent to the subconscious. You will abandon any type of relationship with the rejected part.

That subconscious could also be represented by the part of the iceberg that you don't see. But, to put it in some way, you cannot stay in the subconscious because whatever you have rejected is part of you, so your subconscious will send your rejected part to your conscience, but backward.

How about the reverse?

I explain.

Why does the other's behavior bother you?

Let's continue with the previous example. If weakness is rejected as an emotion, by adults or by society, you will also reject it, and you will not want to know anything about it.

So, two things can happen:

1. You will not be able to recognize weakness in yourself,

but you will be able to see it in others, and you will not bear it.

2. You may be able to recognize weakness in yourself, but you cannot afford it so you will deny and reject it.

And this is how you learn to project onto others those discarded parts of yourself.

Can't stand pushy people?

What if I tell you that one of these two things may be happening to you?

That you have your share of arrogance, but that you are unable to see it or, that you see it, but that you do not allow it, because there is an adverse judgment in your mind that prevents it.

Really, how bad is arrogance or weakness?

From my point of view, it will depend on the situation, the moment, the person in front of you.

Do I need to show strength always?

Can you afford weakness in certain situations?

Can you be pushy with people or situations when necessary?

The two ways to discover your dark side

I've already explained the two ways to you with an example to make it easier to understand, but let's now try to create more parts of your shadow.

To do this, I propose a small exercise:

Find those characteristics, behaviors, or feelings of other people that bother you.

The latter part, "that bother you" is essential because if you do not like these behaviors, but do not move anything inside, they may not have to do with you.

You have to look for those behaviors, emotions, or people that you do not support, that make your blood run down when you see them. The ones that do not leave you indifferent, and there, you will have a clue of something that perhaps you may be rejecting.

Once these behaviors, feelings, or qualities of these people have been located, try to look inside yourself and ask yourself the following question.

That which bothers you, have you ever experienced it in yourself?

And, if so, have you allowed yourself? Have you been able to express it?

Imagine that you have felt it, but you have not allowed it.

Now that you've seen it, could you afford it?

Could you afford to be a little weak or a little pushy?

Could you try to do it today?

Could you accept that part of you?

Integrate your shadow

When you do this exercise, you will be able to see what you have been rejecting, and it will be time to recognize it to integrate it into your consciousness.

As you already know, life is a combination of opposites: there is no night without day, darkness without light, inhalation without exhalation.

So, once you have your list made, it will be time to accept those parts you have discovered and:

1. Re-appropriate the projection: recognize that others are a mirror where you can look at yourself and see both your most positive and negative aspects.

Projection

And although this section tries to discover your dark side, you can also do the exercise to determine your most positive side, trying to make a list of people you admire the most.

Write down those behaviors, feelings, or actions that you value from these people and look for them inside you.

I am sure you will find them because one can only see what it is. And if it resonates in you, then you also possess that quality. If it was not so, you could not see it.

It is essential that you even try to find that positive aspect in yourself, to integrate it as a part of yourself.

2. If you can recognize it, but cannot afford it, the time has come to practice.

If you didn't allow yourself to be weak, give yourself small safe spaces where you can free yourself from the burden of having to "always" be strong.

Don't be afraid, because the more weakness you allow yourself, the more your strength grows.

This is how opposites work; the more you go to one side, the more ability you have to go to the other. Remember that weakness and strength are two sides of the same coin.

I assure you that once you integrate those parts into you, you feel liberated, because you no longer have to fight to avoid having certain feelings and, simply, you use them when it arises or when it is necessary.

CHAPTER 2

THE DARK SIDE OF LAUGHTER

Some Comedians were sad without anyone knowing.

What is behind the humor of some comedians? In 2014 something happened that lifted the hare and shocked half the world: Robin Williams committed suicide in his California flat, hanging himself with a belt.

Robin Williams? The actor, who dedicated himself body and soul to make us laugh and infect us with his tenderness for 63 years, killed himself on a Monday in August.

What even his wife wondered was how he could hide the pain of such magnitude in a spider web built on laughter.

Later, she revealed that Williams stopped living because he could not bear the 'Lewi body dementia' that he suffered, a neurodegenerative disease that causes slow movements, joint stiffness, and sometimes tremor, hallucinations, delusions or abnormal responses to various drugs.

He had the worst of senile dementia and Parkinson's. Also, his whole life was bipolar; he went from laughing to crying in a matter of minutes. However, Williams' case is not at all isolated; many of our favorite actors harbor an unknown inner sadness.

THE SAD CLOWN SYNDROME

A study at the University of Oxford concluded that the personality of comedians presents unusual psychological traits. If analyzed medically; many even have psychosis.

"For many comedians, humor is an escape route. They take something that worries or bothers them and joke about it to try to overcome it. The reward is laughter from the public," said therapist Amy Alpine for BBC Mundo.

And it continues, "besides, depression is the result of a chemical mechanism in the brain. When they are alone, they do not have the rush of adrenaline that they get from being on stage in front of the public. And when you lack that adrenaline, the brain is under the effect of substances causing depression. "

That is why they compensate for the lack of adrenaline with drugs (usually cocaine) to alleviate the sadness of loneliness when they have no one in front to make them laugh.

The comics who were depressed (without your knowing)

The list is almost endless, and we cannot analyze nationality by nationality because we would never end. Unfortunately, many comedians committed suicide, as did Robin: Ray Combs, Micke Dubois, Tony Hancock,

Richard Jeni, Freddie Prinze, Charles Rocket, Doodles Weaver, Drake Sather.

But we are talking not only about a reason for suicide but about the lives of many comedians who today, we all owe more than a laugh.

Williams disguised his sadness as he performed unforgettable scenes such as Mrs. Doubfire vacuuming in the living room, Peter Pan throwing colorful food with the lost children, Adrian Cronau looming "hot weather with thermomedical temperatures" in 'Good morning, Vietnam' ... Long before he was ill, he used drugs and alcohol to silence his depression and dissatisfaction with life; this led to a severe addiction from which he had to rehabilitate several times. Besides, his bipolar disorder made him go from happiness to maximum sadness in a matter of moments.

Humorists: Are sad people the ones who make us laugh?

"Laugh, clown, and everyone will applaud you (...) Laugh, clown, over your broken love!" It is the Vesti la Giubba passage from the famous opera by Leoncavallo, and one of the colossal expressions of a theme that always fascinates and gives morbid: the sad, toxic and crazy background that harlequins or, currently, monologists and humorists have.

The pain that is hidden under laughter and that, according to many, is essential to find the keys that make the public break the box. Sometimes, this grief is a perpetual condition and other times, only the button to activate the humorous feeling of life.

A year ago, the monologist and presenter, Dani Mateo, told El Mundo that he had suffered bullying as a child because of his weight. "Pranking myself helped me socialize." The world was not going well for him, and he had to open a new path with machetes and clicks.

The comedian from Almería, Paco Calavera, who is the author of one of the most lucid disquisitions on the photo-cop, says that humor is a good survival tactic in the school jungle: "I remember that as the youngest of the class, when I suddenly made them laugh a couple of times, they would relax and leave me. If someone makes you laugh, your desire to hit him will stop," he tells Yorokobu.

Calavera remembers some words from the British Ricky Gervais that support the idea of sadness as a fertile bed for laughter. "He has a theory that the good comedian has a bitter and serious view of existence, and that's why he's so good at making people laugh."

The person from Almería embodies, to a certain degree, this paradox: I laugh at fewer things than most people, that's why I look for comedy. Humor, he develops, "is not about having natural grace, it is about being a writer, having a critical view of existence, a political vision in the broadest sense of the word."

Eugenio's odyssey

The documentary Eugenio was presented, in which the slippery, broken, and addicted life of the genius of the one who knows was told. The death of his first wife devastated him. But the same day of the funeral, he traveled to Alicante for a performance. Laughter, that plug.

During a wave of success, when he went from collecting 10,000 pesetas per performance to a million and a half per gala, as reported by El Español, the boat was earthed. His life became a party, one of those sprees that hide the seed of the debacle: he fell into cocaine and chaos.

Days of home disappeared. He had bladder cancer and suffered a heart attack. The excesses. At the dawn of the new century, before he died, he confessed to his son: "I want you to know that I have done very badly. I have made a lot of money, and I have managed it fatally. I have been a bad father ."

It is one of the myriad stories that contrast tragedy and humor. Madness and humor. Or misery, sadness, sickness, antisocial behavior, cruelty, and mood. They are stories that spread well.

This contrast is less surprising in the Catalan joke teller. He was the least clown of the humorists: his proposal consisted of indolence. With Eugenio, it was the other way around: the public was looking at him with a magnifying glass, trying to find in his face a splinter of laughter that would bring him a little closer to people.

There are more seductive cases. Many articles compile these stories in which mythical happy comedians end up revealing themselves, over the years, as broken characters. It's funny: we are a species that left its horns to find gold nuggets in piles of mud, but when it comes to valuing our fellows, we see the dirt within the gold more.

Cases: The silent movie star, Max Linder, when he lost his fame and contracts, plunged into an abyss, ended up drinking Veronal and injecting himself and his wife to end everything. Charles Chaplin, the teacher, the visual poet of laughter, was an unbearable man. The papers of his divorce with Lita Gray described him as "cruel and inhuman." The Spanish Fofito succumbed to alcohol and depression. It twinkled in front of the children, but under his extreme clown grimaces, there was thick pain.

What is right here? Is the connection between comedy and anxiety and trauma indissoluble? Or does it not go beyond what happens in other professions?

Personality disorders as a source of humor?

Headed research by Gordon Claridge, of the Department of Experimental Psychology at Oxford, yielded a disturbing conclusion: "The creative elements needed to produce mood are strikingly similar to those that characterize the cognitive style of people with schizophrenia or bipolar disorder.

The scientist pointed to slight distortions of schizophrenia or manic thinking that could increase expertise in associating unusual and original ideas. Mild: because people with the most pronounced disorder can hardly process the humor.

They compared the questionnaires made to comedians with others made to actors or people with non-creative work. Humorists rated higher on psychotic personality. Common behaviors emerged: disorganized thinking, feeling of failure, guilt, loneliness, significant difficulties off stage, or mood swings.

The Claridge team's results, for some reason, dovetail with these preconceptions. Either because it makes the humorists' personality and crossroads more attractive (and epic), or because they lack limits of many of them when tackling and mocking tricky topics. This pushes us to assume that they don't have both feet in place.

"It is not the first time that I have heard about the tendency to psychopathy. I am surprised by this complex analysis that is made of comedians," reflects Calavera. They are, for him, wanting to look for the B side. "I'm sure there are more psychopathic people among those who write about comedians than among the comedians themselves."

The man from Almería questions this need to analyze and lay a chair on the psyche of humorists. "I do not see studies on other trades that dare to say that they all share certain psychological traits; that thing so violent and almost offensive."

In his opinion, they are always locked into extreme categories: "Or it is said that we are all day laughing and with castanets, which is impossible, there is none that is so; or it is said that we are little less than Jack The Ripper: depressive, manic, not sociable ..."

Calavera's opinion aligns with the results of other investigations that break prejudice and draw a more prosaic and less tasty reality.

Peter McGraw, a professor at the University of Colorado and author of The Humor Code: A Global Search for What Makes Things Funny, explained his findings to Time magazine: "People think that comedians have such dark personalities, but many people have dark characters and most don't become comical. Quite simply, comedians receive a greater focus of attention."

McGraw designed an experiment to learn how humor

conditioned the image that people construct of a person. Participants (humorous and not) wrote two stories, one fun and one interesting. The texts were exposed to other people, who rated the authors of the funny stories as more problematic.

It is the humorous matter itself that seems dissonant, erratic. Maybe that's why we are amused. "Humor plays with taboos. Talk about the wrong things. You have to act foolishly and disclose information that makes you laugh," the author told Times.

Surviving laughter

There is not enough scientific consensus to hold a strong position; There are only some cases that are used when you want to confirm a version of the story and others that are forgotten. But the truth is that there is a point of distinction in the way of looking and verbalizing the comedians. There is a moment in which the humorist premieres brooms of thought that others do not manage to use with the same mastery.

Each era has its ways of undermining the individual, but for all of them, humor seems to work as a strategy of liberation or release.

Miguel Gila also used humor as protection or as a flight strategy. He told it in his biography. After he was shot poorly, Gila waited for the platoon (the enemy) to leave. It was stained with the blood of others. At dawn, he fled.

Later he joined other detainees and began his prison journey. In the Torrijos prison (Madrid), in the middle of the tragedy, he began to draw humorous vignettes.

It would be good to say that Gila went on stage to receive that focus of light so different from the twisted light of the firing bonfires that went up to mitigate the earthy aftertaste that would survive in her mouth since that night of her 19 years. But we don't know if it was so. Maybe he just did it because he was having fun like a kid.

6 SIGNS TO LOCATE A FAKE PERSON

How do you know if a person is genuinely what they say they are? We are going to give clear signs of personalities that, deep down, are not what they seem.

1. They smile... ALL THE TIME

Usually, a smile generates a feeling of warmth, acceptance, and empathy with others.

FAKE: There is something about his smile that makes me uncomfortable.

Did you know there are signs to spot a fake smile?

Authentic smiles are called "Duchenne."

By researcher Guillaume Duchenne

It involves the movement of the significant and minor zygomatic muscles near the mouth and the orbicularis muscle near the eyes.

Duchenne's smile is believed to be produced as an involuntary response to a genuine emotion: it is considered a genuine smile.

Fake smiles:

Open eyes. There are no crow's feet.

Lower teeth exposed (the movement of the cheeks and

223

lips in an authentic smile brings the lips up; discovering the lower teeth is a movement that is done voluntarily).

Without seeing the person's mouth, we can know if it is an authentic smile or not.

2. They Say Who They Are

An authentic person does not have to say who he is: he just shows it. He is aware of the importance of his image to others. However, this is not an obsession, but a natural result of his way of being and acting.

FAKE: They describe themselves; they talk about themselves at the slightest provocation; they need others to know and understand who they "are."

They have an obsessive concern about their public image: it drives them out of control to feel that someone has made them look bad in front of others in any way.

They self-validate and self-affirm recurrently.

3. Confused Compliments

It is normal to throw a flower from time to time; in fact, we have already talked about how it can help in the public image to be aware of small details in others.

FAKE: These confusing compliments can be:

Excessive: you feel that they are irrelevant, that they are

superfluous either because they do not agree with the type of relationship you have with that person, for the moment in which they are made, or for the effusiveness with which they are made.

With a double message: "Oh my god, I love your apartment! It's so small and cute!" "That dress looks so good on you... very flattering in the stomach area."

4. They Are Passive-Aggressive

Confrontation is the basis for the resolution of any conflict between two parties.

FAKE: It is difficult to know what bothers them, or what they think.

These people do not conceive the concept of confrontation. Either they keep quiet about what they think, or they say it with a third party. Which brings us to the next point:

5. They Talk Behind Other's Back

We are all tempted to do it hundreds of times a day; The main difference between an authentic person and one who is not is that the first person can sustain what he says both behind his back and in front of another.

FAKE: Your speech changes if you are forced into a confrontation (which, as we said, this person will avoid at all costs).

6. Iron temper?

Some people are influential and have abilities to channel and control their emotions, so they don't explode, but that doesn't mean they aren't feeling something.

FAKE: They don't get angry, they don't go out of their way, they don't break. EYE: this usually leads to unexpected explosions in which, without their control, their true personality is revealed.

CHAPTER 3

THE ART OF PERSUASION

Persuasion is not just about discovering a person's emotional profile. You have to look for unsatisfied emotions and give them a way out. Listen to what they are concerned about and come up with solutions. Persuasion, in a sense, is also a task that involves creating a desire in others.

Whether it is about closing a deal, asking for a fee increase, motivating a sales team of 5,000 people, negotiating on an individual basis, acquiring a new company, or scrapping an outdated one, situations, contingencies or conjunctures almost always come down to relationship problems and personal treatment.

These unavoidable problems of relationship and personal treatment require, for their correct resolution, persuasive action, since the other paths involve the curtailment of the freedom of others, such as threats, coercion, the use of force, etc.

Persuasion is necessary because individuals, communities, and nations often have different interests, customs, points of view, etc. When the achievement of one person's goals is blocked by the behavior of another in pursuit of their goal, persuasion is used to convince the offender to redefine his goal or modify the means to achieve it.

Persuasion is necessary because there is resistance. To resist is to oppose a force or a body to the action or violence of another force or another body. Many physical phenomena are based on resistance, and thanks to them, we can live. Why do you resist? On the mental plane, resistance is also an inevitable phenomenon: through resistance, we create lasting impressions, impact, persuade, convince, and negotiate.

Resistance, on the psychological plane, is illustrated by the principle of "cognitive dissonance." Psychologists call "cognitive dissonance" the phenomenon by which our minds instinctively reject the possibility of containing two opposing thoughts or beliefs.

Therefore, in our human relationships, we exchange different thoughts, feelings, and hopes that resist each other. That is why all human beings exercise resistance. And when you study why you resist your-self, you understand why others resist.

And that understanding is crucial because it doesn't seem very skillful to combat resistance. As the repetition of the words themselves seems to graph it, it is like "condemning a sentence" or "shouting saying that one should not shout." Resistance must be allowed to flow, that is, it must be allowed its full expression, even allowing it to reach its limit.

The resistance is moderated with "lubricants," with "shock absorbers," listening and giving space to the

228

other. Resistance is a thought, almost always accompanied by a feeling. By subtly changing that thought, resistance can disappear.

The First Element of Persuasion is nothing but influence. And influence begins with what matters to your potential ally. Professor Harry Overstreet, in his illustrative book *Influencing Human Behavior*, says: "Action arises from what we fundamentally desire (...) and the best advice that can be given to those who seek to be persuasive, whether in business, at home, in school or politics is this: first, to awaken in the neighbor a frank desire. Whoever can do this has the whole world with him—those who cannot walk alone along the way. Therefore, the strength of mutual exchange consists in obtaining what one wants and giving others what they need."

Persuasion is a mere intellectual exercise: How to persuade is to make the feelings and ideas that we would like them to have appear in the spirit of one or more other people. And we must always keep in mind that our actions do not only come from abstract reasons, cultural guidelines, etc. They mainly come from our desires, interests, and emotions.

"If I could describe in one sentence the art of persuasion, that phrase would be the following: persuasion is to convert people, not in our way of thinking, but in our way of feeling and believing."

People do things for emotional reasons. Therefore,

persuading is also influencing the emotional attitudes of others.

Already from ancient Greece, Aristotle was concerned with finding an adequate definition of what we understood by rhetoric, defining it as "the art of discovering, in each particular case, the adequate means for persuasion." This concern remains until today when the ability to convince has become a highly desired art to obtain an excellent performance in our labor and social relations.

Currently, the ability to persuade is strongly linked to the term 'persuasion,' understood as a process aimed at modifying a person's behavior or beliefs through the use of arguments or feelings. That is why having a high trait of persuasion is considered as one of the main factors to increase the chances of convincing others of our arguments significantly.

Characteristics of the persuasive person

Persuasive people share several characteristics that, among other things, increase their ability to convince others. Among them we can highlight:

They are friendly in relation to others: they are easy-going people who are close, making interaction a pleasant moment.

They are aware of the needs and limitations of others: this fact allows them to choose interesting arguments that make their interlocutor feel understood. This is a capacity that makes them believe that if they follow their instructions, their needs will be met.

They handle non-verbal communication, theirs, and that of their interlocutor: rarely does a persuasive person not speak to you with a smile and kind gestures. At the same time, they know how to read in you your needs, emotional states, and the effects that what they are saying has on you.

They study their message, calculating exactly what information you are interested in knowing, not providing you with more or fewer details than necessary.

They are charismatic in relation to others: this aspect makes us want to be like them and therefore follow their attitudes and way of thinking.

They have credibility for the interlocutor: they are people worthy of respect and trust on the part of the people whom they convince, who think that it would be well for them to be like them.

They have authority for the listener: the way of exercising persuasion from authority is not so desirable since from here, the line between the persuasive and the coercive person is blurred. However, there are people who use the scare method to convince others, albeit from a more aggressive position.

The five fundamental principles to master the art of persuasion.

Persuasion is an art. As such, it requires effort and perseverance to master yourself. The interesting thing is that its applications in your life are practically unlimited.

It doesn't matter if you are leading a group; you are selling a project idea or trying to convince your children; the ability to persuade is essential to achieve this in all cases. If you also reach it without appearing stubborn and insistent, so much the better. Well, that will guarantee that you will persuade them again in the future.

Of course, you are trying to persuade for your own purposes ... But it is vital to understand the motivations of the other, as well as to follow these steps:

1. MAKE THE BENEFIT IMMEDIATE

People care about fast, tangible results. Don't tell them that things will improve "30% in a few weeks," tell them that they will start to see a 2% improvement daily starting today.

You are offering the same, but the immediacy of the second version will be more seductive.

2. MAKE IT PERSONAL

In addition to immediacy, people like the benefits of being self-directed, even when searching for the solution for someone else.

For example, the seller of a construction toy does not have to convince the child to own it but to convince the parents that this activity will develop their child's spatial intelligence (and keep them busy for a long time). That will make them feel like they are better parents ... And it will give them quiet time!

And when you have to persuade a group of people...

3. USE YOUR AUDIENCE'S VALUES (EVEN IF THEY DON'T HAVE THEM)

A persuasive person forgets what he needs for a moment. He even tries to go beyond what the other person needs and aim for what he wants. There is a big difference!

For example, you may need to motivate a group of colleagues to undertake a project with which they do not strongly agree. Tell them that "I know they don't exactly like this project ... (recognize the situation), but I'm sure their combined skills are ideal for completing it beyond perfection."

First, you recognize the situation, then you realize their abilities (and the need to combine them), and you appeal to their aspiration: to work as a team (a longing recurrently exploited in all kinds of fiction), beyond the simple fulfillment of duty.

4. UNDERSTAND YOUR COMPETITION

To understand is to identify, understand, and absorb at the same time. Once you know what your competitors offer, you have two options: either exploit their weaknesses by highlighting your strengths or choose a lateral route...

Domino´s pizza did it when it was on the verge of bankruptcy: they were not the best pizzeria (there were at least 30 better or cheaper pizzerias in their city). So the premise they used was the simple "Your pizza in 30 minutes ... Or it's free." It was no longer the taste nor the price, just the convenience of guaranteed service.

5. BE REAL AND AUTHENTIC

You may be on the verge of acceptance, signing the contract, yes ... And to encourage it, you promise (or just speak!) more than you should. At that critical moment, it is better to sin by default than by excess. You run the risk of exaggerating the virtues of what you propose, affecting the confidence that you had developed until then.

For example, if the person covers his mouth in a reflective attitude, let the idea "cooks" alone in his mind, and in any case, invite him to ask any question he wants.

The art of persuading with respect and wisdom

There is no doubt that persuasion is an art. It seems that some are born with this gift. However, it is a myth. You too can learn how to persuade others.

It is also essential to differentiate between selling and persuading. Overcoming implies struggle and confrontation with another person. Still, if we act with respect and wisdom, we will understand that overcoming is only something that satisfies our ego and that we don't need it. It is necessary to find and have the wisdom so that our objective is not to win but to convince and persuade another person to do what we want because they want to.

Techniques to persuade

One of the tools that can be used to persuade someone is reverse psychology, a behavioral technique used by the psychiatrist and writer Viktor Frankl.

Reverse psychology is about modifying a person's behavior by telling them to do what we don't want them to do. That is, with this technique, we help ourselves from the opposite aspects with the intention that the person rejects our suggestion and does what we want.

In this way, the person will resist taking orders and end up doing what we want. Therefore, the technique works due to what is called "psychological resistance," which occurs when they tell us something that we think may be a limit to our freedom and our ability to decide.

On the other hand, researchers at Yale University, among others Hovland and McGuire, developed a study on persuasion. They concluded that for a persuasive message to change attitude and behavior, it must first change the thoughts or beliefs of the recipient of the message. This change will take place whenever the receiver receives different ideas from his, accompanied by incentives.

There are four critical elements in the persuasion process.

The effectiveness of a persuasive message will depend on them, and they are the following: the source, the content of the message, the communication channel, and the context.

How can you persuade others?

The art of persuading is a complex learning process that includes many factors such as intelligence, empathy, humor, sincerity, respect, the real will to approach positions to reach an agreement ... Therefore, we are going to comment on some of the secrets of the art of persuading with intelligence and respect.

1. Sincerity

The source of the persuasive message is related to sincerity. In other words, the source must be seen as credible and true for the message to be sincere. It is good to consider our interlocutor as an intelligent person who will know whether or not our message is sincere. You should not use testimonies or fabricated facts. If your interlocutor catches you in resignation, you and each of your messages will have lost all credibility.

2. The right time

For our message to be effective and persuasive, the choice of when we are going to communicate is essential. On the other hand, we mustn't use too many decorations so that the main message can be lost. It is also necessary to know how to manage silences and to be silent when we must be silent.

3. The experience of others

The third element is based on the importance of considering the value of other people's honest testimonies. Many companies today have achieved their success based on the testimonials and experiences of others.

What a third party or user of a company says is more credible than what that company says about itself. That is why collaborative companies based on user opinions and mutual collaboration are increasingly developed.

4. Persuade thanks to reciprocity

It is the last fundamental element of persuasion. If we receive something, we will feel indebted to the person who gave it to us. That is why in marketing, the technique of delivering free samples is used to attract customers, or in spy movies we see in many scenes as the protagonist, to gain someone's trust, try to give him something, even if it is a stick.

But in this sense, it is necessary to take into account who the person we are dealing with is and to know what their needs are. In this way, we will create an environment of reciprocity and exchange in order to intelligently exercise persuasion.

The art of persuading is not a gift of birth. On the contrary, people who pay attention to the needs and interests of others can come to convince them with empathy and with messages and actions that encourage others to follow them, since their messages coincide with the other's goals or ambitions.

Persuasion is the social influence of beliefs, attitudes, intentions, motivations, and behaviors.

1. Persuasion is a process intended to change the attitude or behavior of a person or group towards some event, idea, object or person (s), by using words to convey information, feelings, or reasoning, or a combination of them.

2. It is the process of guiding people towards the adoption of an idea, attitude, or action through rational and symbolic meanings (although not always logical). It is a problem-solving strategy that relies on "requests" rather than coercion. According to Aristotle's statement, "rhetoric is the art of discovering, in each particular case, the proper means of persuasion."

Have someone adopt a way of thinking or acting through the use of arguments, whether they change their thoughts and opinions into beliefs or methods of seeing life.

PERSUASION METHODS

Persuasion methods are sometimes also called persuasion tactics or persuasion strategies.

According to Robert Cialdini in his book Psychology of Persuasion, there are six weapons of influence:

Reciprocity

People tend to return a favor. Hence the persuasion of free samples in marketing and advertising. In his lectures, Cialdini often uses the example of Ethiopia who provided thousands of dollars for humanitarian aid to Mexico just after the 1985 earthquake, despite Ethiopia then suffering from severe famine and engulfed civil war. It happened since Ethiopia had reciprocally received diplomatic support from Mexico when Italy invaded it in 1937.

Commitment and consistency

On a beach in New York, the following drill was developed to verify this principle, and, in the first scenario, a radio was purposely left on a towel, and a "false thief" was asked to pass and very shamelessly carried it away. The purpose, in this case, was to establish how many people would be able to risk stopping the robbery. Only 4 out of 20 people did.

Then, a small change was made to the experiment, and the results changed dramatically; on the second stage and before the "robbery," the person who owned the radio asked the bathers around him to watch his things while he returned. In that case, the bathers, who were now under the effect of the principle of commitment and consistency, adopted an active vigilance position. The result is that 19 out of 20 people actively tried to stop the robbery.

Of course, commitment and consistency must be preceded by an initial action of response or promise, and their power is greatly increased if the agreement is given in writing. For example, if by email we say: "Last week you told us you wanted XYZ, well, it happens that here you have it!"

The social proof

People will do those things that they see other people doing. For example, in an experiment, if one or more participants look up at the sky, then the other people present will also look up to see what others have seen at the time. When this experiment was carried out, so many people looked up that they created traffic.

The authority

Individuals would continue to follow figures of authority, particularly if they are called upon to do unpleasant things. Cialdini cites events such as the early 1960s Milgram experiments and the assassination of M. Lai.

Taste

People are easily convinced by other people with whom they feel comfortable. Cialdini cites Tupperware marketing, which can now be called viral marketing. People buy more comfortably if they like the person who is selling the product. Some of the trends that favor attractive people are discussed, but generally, aesthetically pleasing people tend to use this influence on others with great results.

Shortage

The perceived shortage will generate demand. For example, those offers that claim to be available for "a limited time" thus encourage consumption.

The propaganda is also closely related to persuasion. It is the set of messages aimed at influencing the opinion or behavior of a large number of people. The information you present is not impartial but seeks to influence the audience. Although the information offered is often true, the facts are presented selectively, to encourage a particular synthesis or provoke a more emotional than rational response to the information presented. The term 'propaganda' first appeared in 1622, when Pope Gregory XV created the Sacred Congregation for the Propagation of the Faith. Originally, as today, propaganda sought to convince as many people as possible about the veracity of a set of ideas. Propaganda is as old as people.

Kurt Mortensen is another Author who also detailed very neatly how to apply tactics during persuasion. In his book The Art of Influencing Others, he classifies different persuasion strategies according to their duration over time. In this way, the control strategy based on force, fear, and threat is effective but only in the short term. On the other hand, the most lasting and sustained influence over time is that of commitment based on respect, honor, and trust.

Mortensen increases his weapons of persuasion and describes how to persuade on 12 main fundamentals:

1. The law of dissonance: People usually have a greater tendency to follow and gravitate towards people who are consistent in their behavior.

2. The law of obligation or reciprocity: When others do something for us, we feel a strong need, even pressure, to return the favor.

3. The law of connectivity: The more connected we feel with someone or feel more part of someone, or when we like or attract someone, the more persuasive we find them.

4. The law of social validation: We tend to change our perceptions, opinions, and behaviors in accordance and coherently with the norms of the group. We consider that the behavior is more correct when we see that other people have it.

5. The Law of Scarcity: Opportunities are always more valuable and exciting when they are scarce and less available.

6. The law of verbal wrapping: The more skillful a person is at using language, the more persuasive he will be. The author includes a quote from Jim Rohn that says that true persuasion comes from putting more of you into everything you say. Words have an effect. Words full of emotion have a powerful effect.

7. The law of contrast: When we are presented with two completely different alternatives in succession, in general, if the second option is very different from the first, we tend to see it even more different than it actually is.

8. The law of expectations: A person tends to make decisions based on how others expect him to act.

9. The Law of Involvement: The more you attract someone's five senses, and the more you involve them mentally and physically and create the right environment for persuasion, the more effectiveness and persuasion you will achieve.

10. The Law of Valuation: All people need and want praise, recognition, and acceptance.

11. The law of association: To maintain order in the world, our brain relates objects, gestures, and symbols to our feelings, memories, and life experiences. Masters of persuasion take advantage of association to evoke corresponding positive thoughts and feelings to the message they are trying to convey.

12. The law of balance: When persuading, you must focus your message on the emotions, while maintaining the balance between logic and feelings.

Relationship

-Based on Persuasion.

G. Richard Shell and Moussa Mario present a four-stage approach to strategic persuasion in their book The Art of Woo. They clarify that convincing requires winning over and not overcoming others. Therefore, in order to predict the reaction that others have to a suggestion, it is important to be able to see the topic from various angles.

Step 1 - Take a look at the situation.

Each phase requires an overview of the situation, priorities, and obstacles the persuader faces within the organization.

Step 2 - Face the five barriers.

Five obstacles pose the greatest risks for a successful influence encounter: relationships, credibility, communication mismatches, belief systems, interests, and needs.

Step 3 - Make your tone.

People need a compelling reason to justify a decision, yet at the same time, many of the decisions are made on the basis of intuition. This step also addresses presentation skills.

Step 4 - Secure your commitments.

In order to safeguard the long-term success of a persuasive decision, it is vital to deal with politics, both at the individual and organizational levels.

CHAPTER 4

MANIPULATIVE PEOPLE HAVE THESE 5 TRAITS IN COMMON

How can we protect ourselves from being manipulated by someone?

Surely, on some occasion, you will have met a person who has convinced you of what suits you. But in time, it turned out that what, according to them, suits you is a ring to the finger and in the end, you fall into the realization that what you are doing is not your desire.

Manipulative men, and their vices.

Such people have no qualms when they ask you to set your desires aside for the benefit of everyone. They are men who don't even thank you when they receive what they want from you.

These people also receive the name of manipulators, and sadly society is full of them. They are very likely to make you question your ability by feeling weak or inferior to others. They're reinforced by the potential they have to manipulate others' values as they draw you to their playing field, telling you that you can't do it or that you can do it in their own way because they are the ones who know how things are going.

Their strength lies in emotional exploitation (and emotional blackmail); that is, they manage your emotions, producing a feeling of guilt, completely unfounded guilt, and that gives rise to you giving in to their desires.

How are the manipulators?

So, in this way, the manipulators gain control by finding their prey reward and also in a calculated way. In this section, we will try to identify manipulative attitudes to curb them.

1. They're trained in finding other people's vulnerabilities

We all have vulnerabilities, and these are the weapons they use to manipulate you. And if you refuse to believe, there's something that makes you feel guilty, and you want to hide. The malicious individual can seek to find this out, so if the chance occurs, he will use it against you.

2. They do not stop until they achieve what they want

They have few qualms about stepping on somebody, and the result justifies the means for them. When they go to act, they don't hesitate to do what's needed to accomplish their goals; despite all this, their actions always go unnoticed because they are good actors.

3. They are insatiable

Manipulation makes them feel powerful, and, as is often the case with power, they always want more. Their moral principles are somewhat damaged, as they are aware that they are incapable of reaching a goal by themselves, but that their manipulative capacity can provide them to reach their goal using the merits of others, behind the backs of others. Their ambition fills them, a craving that, like a drug, produces a kind of addiction.

4. They need control

The manipulator usually suffers from the so-called superiority complex; They are usually people with traits close to egocentrism and narcissism. They like to outdo themselves and outperform the previous level, looking for ever greater challenges.

Nevertheless, people who feel the need to find themselves superior to others, even perfect beings, thriving by other people's merits, denote some weakness that is clothed with the appearance of strength. But deep down, they conceal an immense fear that they are poor.

Are all handlers the same?

Because manipulation is an art, we may assume that the gift of manipulation consists of various capacities and skills, under this category, different types of manipulators can be identified.

1. The Promoter

A typical case contrary to the previous two listed. The promoter flaunts power, not just a certain aggressiveness. In this case, if you're a passive person, you're going to give in to avoid having to face that person. In this way, the manipulator achieves "ad baculum" through coercion, what he desires is the case for antisocial personalities.

2. The debunker that is

The narcissism of this type of manipulator is specially marked. It just feels good, and it is a blackbird white, it has never broken a piece. He's the indicator of things, and the only thing that matters is his law. This "complete gift" would reinforce that you're wrong if you say something, whenever he's given the opportunity. This manipulator will bring out your flaws and mock you with his sarcasm. They are people who devote themselves to judging others but usually don't look in the mirror because they don't want to compliment themselves.

3. The interpreter

This particular type is especially harmful when it comes to a group of people, whether it be work or family. He has a Machiavellian and twisted personality, and acts by extracting your words and changing their meaning, a meaning intentionally different from the message that you wanted to communicate.

With this trick, he will make you wish you had swallowed your words, that they were not appropriate, that you were over the line. Or that you did not think what you were saying was hurting someone else—metamorphosing your words in this way, communicating them to the person who best suits you and modifying their intention, so you can end up being the bad guy in the movie.

4. The victim

He never stops lamenting that something negative is happening to him and asking himself, "Why me?" He focuses more on his own suffering, hiding under victimhood his reprehensible behaviors. He's still the unhappiest, well above the rest. This kind of mental perception is also called Work syndrome.

Moreover, it leads one to believe that others exploit him. He seeks justice, and he sees himself as a victim mistreated, thereby building a debate such that you feel guilty of his suffering and how unjust life is to him. A universe that is with him. So, they typically take advantage of that speech to lower your defense and push you out of sympathy or shame to submit to what they are asking for. You'll be frustrated later because it's not what you really wanted, but by his complaining, he's already accomplished his goal.

5. The remora that is

This sort of manipulator makes use of your own ego. He's able to make you feel superior; he's less than nothing next to you, a frail and incompetent guy, and of course unable to do something while you're doing. And you're going to end up doing what he can't do.

The commiseration creates inside you, and your own power ego will compel you, unconsciously, to do what the manipulator does not want to do. In this way, yours will be the consequence of such exercise without receiving more compensation than the hollow sensation of energy, which in addition to the consequent fatigue, will later become a waste of time.

How to guard ourselves against this form of person?

As we have shown, there are various kinds of manipulators. Now, what steps can we take to keep ourselves from falling victim to their psychological games?

1. Be conscious

The first thing we have to do is become aware of the exploitation. There are inviolable and non-transferable rights, and those rights are: to be treated with dignity.

- For setting your own goals.
- To voice your opinion and to voice how you feel.

- For physically or emotionally protecting yourself.
- To say "no" without having to feel guilty.
- When you work with others and believe they are breaching your rights, understand that you might be the target of a manipulator.

2. Hold distance to safety

Keep a safe distance mentally, just as we keep a safe distance when driving, so we don't run into another car and save ourselves an accident. To stop being hunted, don't let someone enter your space or touch your spider web. Without your permission, no one can harm you.

3. You shouldn't blame them

If you answer no to all of the above questions, assume that you might be the perpetrator and not the other way around. There are many facets of nature that affect you, and you should exercise power over them. Most of the issues are not in our possession, though, so you're not to blame for what's happening around you, and if you start feeling like that, try to figure out what's happening.

Question:

- Do you think what you are asking for is fair?
- Why do I want to tell you, in your opinion?
- You ask me, or you'll tell me?

Issues such as these will lead you to consider the dishonest subject which has been deceived and is likely to be searching for someone else to dupe.

4. Grab your moment

Right before you need to think, don't respond to their demands. The manipulators also place pressure on their victims so that they don't stop fulfilling their demands. Understanding how to identify these moments is important in order not to allow the power of the moment to succumb to reason and to let others' interests pass us by.

5. Make no hesitation

Do not hesitate in your convictions and remain firm in your claims. When reading the non-verbal interactions, the manipulators are very professional because they assume, they can understand it and apply more pressure before they eventually give in.

CHAPTER 5

PATHOS, ETHOS AND LOGOS: THE RHETORIC OF ARISTOTLE

In Aristotle's rhetoric, logos is the most prominent type of rhetoric. It refers to logical reasoning, to our attempt to make use of the intellect.

When we present our arguments, whether oral or written, we try to be persuasive. Just before accepting our claims, the public must consider our point of view. That is what rhetoric is; that others adopt our point of view.

So, who better to explain rhetoric than Aristotle? Plato's student studies focused on rhetoric. For this reason, Aristotle's rhetoric consists of three categories: pathos, ethos, and logos.

In Aristotle's rhetoric, pathos, ethos, and logos are the three fundamental pillars. Today, these three categories are considered different ways of convincing an audience about a particular topic, belief, or conclusion. Let's delve into the topic below.

Aristotle's pathos

Pathos means trauma and pain. This is Aristotle's rhetoric that brings with it the power of the speaker or writer to elicit emotions and feelings in his audience. Emotion is connected with the pathos, it helps to empathize with the viewer, and it stimulates the imagination.

Essentially, pathos needs collective empathy. As used, the ideals, convictions, and knowledge of the arguer are engaged and conveyed via a narrative to the viewer. Therefore, according to studies such as those conducted by doctors Frans Derkse and Jozien Bensing, at Nijmegen University in Norway, empathy is crucial to improving not only contact but the relation between people from an emotional perspective.

The pathos is used when the claims being put forward are divisive. Because certain claims are often lacking in reasoning, the ability to empathize with the audience would be successful.

In an argument for legally banning abortion, for instance, descriptive metaphors may be used to portray babies and the promise of a new life to cause sorrow and concern on the part of the public.

The religion of Aristoteles

The second type, ethos, means morality and is derived from the word ethnos, which means spiritual and moral morality. The ethic is influenced by its reputation and audience resemblance for speakers and authors. As an authority on the subject, the speaker must be trustworthy and respected. Trustworthy information needs to be delivered accurately as well.

It is not enough to make rational reasoning for the arguments to be successful.

Ethos is especially important in generating public interest according to Aristotle's rhetoric. The message sound and style will be crucial to that.

Additionally, the character can also be affected by the prestige of the argumentation, which is independent of the message.

Talking to an audience as an individual rather than as passive characters, for example, increases the probability that people will actually listen to the arguments.

The Logos of Aristotle

Logos means word, spoken word, or explanation. Convincingly, the logos is the rational rationale behind claims by the speaker. The logos refer to every effort, logical arguments, to appeal to the intellect. Logical reasoning thus presents two forms: inductive and deductive.

Deductive logic suggests that "if A is true and B is true, then the intersection of A and B must also be valid." For instance, the logos statement of "women like oranges" will be "women like fruits" and "oranges are fruits."

Inductive reasoning often uses assumptions, but the inference is merely a belief, and because of its subjective existence may not actually be valid. For instance, the phrases "Peter likes comedy" and "This film is a comedy" may fairly infer that "Peter likes this film."

Aristotle's rhetoric

In Aristotle's rhetoric, logos was his favorite argumentative technique. However, on a day-to-day basis, everyday arguments depend more on pathos and ethos. The combination of all three is used to make rehearsals more persuasive and central to the discussion team's strategy.

The people who master them have the ability to convince others to perform a certain action or to buy a product or service. Even so, in modernity, the pathos seems to have a greater influence. Populist discourses, which seek to excite rather than provide logical arguments, seem to be catching on more easily.

The same is true for fake news. Some even lack logic, but the public accepts them given their great ability to empathize. Being aware of these three strategies of Aristotle's rhetoric can help us to better understand those messages that are only intended to persuade us through fallacies.

What are Ethos, Pathos, and Logos?

In a moment, I will tell you the meaning of ethos, pathos, and logos, and I will also give you several examples. But before starting, keep in mind that this content is considered the ideal when we talk about persuasive discourses. It is not necessary for all kinds of speeches.

That said, the reality is that the vast majority of speeches or presentations are persuasive. Often you are looking for a change in your audience either in behavior or thought, and that is precisely what persuasion means.

Ethos

Ethos refers to the credibility that you may have as a speaker or disseminator. Why should your audience believe what you say?

How would you feel if Luis Bárcenas gave you a speech about honesty and good practices?

In order to persuade your audience, the first thing you need to do is wrap yourself in an aura of credibility. If they do not see you as someone to trust, it does not matter how well structured your arguments are or how rich your non-verbal language is, since it will be very difficult for you to convince them.

Three ways to build Ethos

The first way to do this is to have an ethos built in advance of your reputation. You may be an expert in the subject you are talking about, and you have an academic title that legitimizes you or a trophy that shows you have mastered the discipline you explain.

Imagine that the last Nobel Prize winner in Economics comes to give you a talk about the future of investments in this country. Will you heed to what he says?

The third technique is born from your coherence as a speaker. Your rhetoric, your movements, and the ability to connect with the public are factors that help reinforce your Ethos.

Can you imagine a speaker who stutters, goes blank, and moves nervously around the stage?

It doesn't look good.

Pathos

Pathos refers to the ability of your words to generate emotions in the audience.

Have you ever got goosebumps when listening to a movie speech? Many actors from Russell Crowe to Chaplin have done it. And it is not only for their fantastic interpretation but for the studied text that they are able to touch the most sensitive fibers. And if you add visuals, prepare the scarves.

Appealing to emotions is one of the most powerful resources a speaker has. And one of the most difficult to master.

Three ways to build pathos

The first and most powerful is to show vulnerability.

When someone comes out to speak in front of dozens or hundreds of people and is able to open up and tell something that makes them vulnerable, they are driving on the highway that leads to the hearts of others.

The second strategy is to tell stories. Personal stories or anecdotes make us seem more human and help connect with the public.

When you count the problems, you have had to park in the center of Madrid, you stop being "the speaker" and become a normal person like the rest of the public.

The third strategy is to use metaphors. Metaphors are analogies that explain complicated concepts through simpler stories.

The bible is full of metaphors as well as our popular culture. Tales like the ugly duckling or the ant and the cicada are different ways of explaining a concept. And it is just as Jorge Bucay says: "Tales serve to put children to sleep and wake adults up."

The same thing happens with metaphors.

Logos

Logos refers to the world of logic and reasoning. It is everything that reinforces your message from the prism of reason.

Imagine that you want to talk about how pollution damages our lives.

You could give percentages of pollution in different cities, show graphics, and you could define what is considered pollution: car smoke, some toxic waste, depending on which gases in the industry, etc.

With this, you would be able to give a solid base to your speech and appeal to the analytical part of your audience.

Three ways to build logos

The first is to include graphics or statistics in your speech.

When someone sees a graph that demonstrates a trend or a statistic that supports a statement, their left brain is activated and approves of what you are saying.

The second is to use research, studies, or experiments that address the topic you are dealing with from a scientific perspective. The scientific method has brought many advances in society and is, to this day, the test that all reasoning or theory must pass in order for the majority of the population to adopt it as true.

The third is to show demonstrable facts. I can say that two plus two is four to exemplify a concept, and with it, I use the logic of a demonstrable fact for the entire audience.

You could also say that FC Barcelona was founded in 1899 or that Real Madrid has 11 European cups.

Data, demonstrable facts. Logos.

Ethos, pathos, and logos: all in one

One of my favorite speeches is the one that Robert Kennedy gave in 1968 warning of the danger of measuring the progress and well-being of a nation by its Gross Domestic Product.

CHAPTER 6

NLP (NEURO-LINGUISTIC PROGRAMMING)

Neurolinguistic Programming is a discipline that tries to explain how our brain works and defines its mental patterns. It facilitates our knowledge of ourselves and allows us to change them using certain techniques with the aim of optimizing our communication capacity.

By learning how we process information, we can discover our patterns and change them with certain specific techniques, such as visualization, reframing, timeline, history change, etc.

Through Neurolinguistic Programming (NLP), we become aware of language and the importance of its proper use. It gives us the key to communicate effectively in our personal relationships, and it also helps us break our limitations and achieve profound and lasting changes in us.

What is Neurolinguistic Programming

Neurolinguistic Programming (NLP) is a dynamic model that tries to explain how the human brain works and how we process the information that comes to us from the world around us. With neurolinguistic programming, we discover how the human being communicates with himself and with his environment.

In this way, by learning how we process information, we can discover our patterns and change them with certain specific techniques, such as visualization, reframing, timeline, history change, etc.

NLP origins

It was developed by Richard Bandler (computer scientist and psychotherapist) and John Grinder (university professor of linguistics) in the 1970s at the University of Santa Cruz in California.

They wondered why there were teachers that had a full class and that their students loved attending, while others, with the same level of knowledge, did not transmit and did not achieve such success in attendance. To find out the reason for this situation, they began to "model" people who were "excellent" in their profession. Extraordinary communicators and therapists, such as Virginia Satir, a pioneer in Family Systemic Therapy; Milton Erickson, creator of Ericksonian hypnosis, a pioneer in Clinical Hypnosis; Fritz Perls, Creator of Gestalt Therapy and Gregory Bateson, anthropologist and pioneer in social and verbal sciences.

Through this research, they began to systematize similar mental patterns and identified, in that group of people, patterns of excellence so that they could be used by anyone else and thus obtain similar results.

This discipline was called Neurolinguistic Programming for the following reasons:

Programming: for mathematics and cybernetics, because we are programmed by our memories and learning, by our experiences and beliefs. We have mental programs and behavior patterns.

Neuro: by neurology, because we can deactivate these programs executed by neural networks and activate other more positive programs.

Linguistics: due to the importance of the use of language and its linguistic metamodels (a system of questions that allow for a deeper understanding of the person and their patterns).

They used the modeling technique—observation and systematization of processes—to recreate these specific successful behaviors. They systematized the patterns so that anyone can learn them and reach similar successful results.

The linguistic metamodel of NLP

Bandler and Grinder wrote the first NLP book in 1975 "The Structure of Magic," in which they developed their theory of the aforementioned Language Metamodel (a series of basic syntactic patterns that identify expressions of verbal communication that can limit our reality).

This metamodel, also called precision model, which will allow us, through language, to deepen the knowledge of the person and their mental map, consists of 12 patterns that are divided into three categories:

- Omissions.
- Distortions.
- Information generalizations.

Omissions

We are selective; we pay attention to some of the information, and we discard another part that we think is not important.

Distortions

We understand the information according to our own map, and many times we change it and misunderstand it.

Generalizations

We draw general conclusions based on previous experiences to understand reality. They are the basis of the basic learning processes.

Representational systems

From the perspective of Neurolinguistic Programming, there are three ways of perceiving the world and processing information, which are called representation systems. These are:

Visual: corresponds to people who pay special attention to visual details and, therefore, their memories take the form of images. They need the visual contact of their interlocutor, and since their thoughts emerge in the form of images, they tend to speak quickly and frequently, jumping quickly from the topic. (Circular system).

Auditory: In this case, hearing people tend to remember words and sound better, so their own language is influenced by auditory terms. (Linear system).

Kinesthetic: this system is used by people whose memories come from sensations (body, taste, smell, touch, ...) and, therefore, use physical contact a lot. In this case, as in the previous ones, his own language is influenced by terms that represent sensations. (Network system).

Although we usually use all the senses when processing information, we have a preferential representational system, that is, we think using, to a greater extent, one of the three previous systems. This is the basis of our World Map and our communication.

When we understand what representational system another person is using, we will be able to communicate better and adapt to their language (verbal and non-verbal) to make everything easier and more fluid.

Operational presuppositions or NLP paradigms

NLP is based on a series of presuppositions or paradigms (beliefs) that if we take them as if they were true, they help us to optimize our reality and our relationships with others.

There are numerous presuppositions or paradigms, and depending on the author, they give more relevance to some than to others. In my opinion, the most notable are:

- The map is not the territory (that is, our model of the world, which we have created through our senses and language, corresponds to a partial and personal representation of reality).
- Mind and body are part of the same system.
- A person can communicate.
- People have two levels of communication: conscious and unconscious.
- All the information we receive passes through the five senses.
- To know the answers, it is essential to have clean and open sensory channels.
- All behavior is adaptation oriented.
- We more easily accept what is known.
- The value of your communication is found in the response you receive.
- The most flexible person has the most influence on the system.

- Rapport is the meeting of people in the same model of the world.
- All behavior has a positive intention.
- People have all the necessary resources to make any changes they want.
- If what you've done so far doesn't work, do something else.
- There are no failures or errors in communication, only results.
- Change produces change.
- If it's possible for someone, it's possible for me.
- The importance of connecting with the interlocutor: rapport

Rapport is a basic tool in the techniques that make NLP, and they have to do with generating a good feeling and connection while communicating with another person.

This technique, therefore, allows us to try to influence our interlocutor, to provoke that good connection and empathy that favors the communication process and the feeling of comfort on both sides.

To achieve this rapport, we use a multitude of aspects such as, for example, breathing, gestures and body postures, tone and speed of the voice, representational systems (visual, auditory, kinesthetic), facial expressions and movements, distance etc.

We must divide this process into two steps:

- Calibrate
- Accompany

First, we will calibrate bodily, taking special attention in:

- The breathing
- The gestures
- The postures

Define what representational system our interlocutor is using (we observe their eye movements, the characteristics of the voice, the structure of the message, the predicates, the perceptual position...).

When we already have all the data, we go to pacing:

- Corporal: direct or mirrored
- Language predicates
- We use the representational system you are using

When we match, we must do it subtly, learning to observe the micro-movements and behaviors of the person to calibrate (observe). Rapport is established when we synchronize our non-verbal and verbal language with the person in front of us. And that we want him to modify something (we have a specific objective, or the person himself has it if what we are in is, for example a Coaching session with a client). When we subtly change our language the other person also changes it, that means that the rapport has been established.

To check if the rapport is working, we can subtly change our body posture, for example, crossing our legs to the other side and checking if the person is following us.

Uses of NLP

With NLP, we can make big and lasting changes.

Today NLP is used in many techniques of personal development such as Coaching and in many areas of everyday life such as Human Resources, sales, conflict resolution, education, etc.

The name of Neuro-linguistic Programming consists of three terms:

Programming: It is a term that refers to the organization's processes of the components of a system. It refers to the established mental programs that govern our thinking and behavior, which we can program in a similar way to how a computer would be programmed to perform certain functions that interest us.

Neuro: Which comes from the Greek "Neuron" and says that all behavior is the result of a neurological process. All action or behavior is a function of the neurological activity set in motion from the information that comes to us through the senses. The interpretation that we give to said information is the one that shapes our perception of the world around us.

Linguistics: This is derived from the Latin "Lingua" and indicates that the neurological process is represented, ordered, sequenced, and transmitted through communication based on word or language. It recognizes the part that language occupies as a representation of our mental organization and our operational strategies.

NLP: The tool that facilitates the achievement of objectives.

When we talk about Neuro-linguistic Programming (NLP), everyone evokes the way a computer works: based on the data we enter and the program we work with, the machine processes, stores, and updates the information every time it is used. In our case, the data entered would be the sensory information that we continuously receive from the outside: everything we see, hear, taste, feel, etc. It is processed and stored based on the programming we have in our brain and based on that programming, we give it meaning.

When we find ourselves in a situation that resembles others previously lived, our brain compares the data that we are receiving at that moment with that stored in our memory from previous situations. And the reaction that we will have in the present will depend on the meaning that we had previously provided such data.

For example, if, as a child, your teacher gave you a hard time every time he took you to the board and your classmates laughed at you, you ended up associating public speaking with a distressing situation, and therefore, it became something to avoid. So if even a few years after the school incident, someone invites you to give a lecture, it is possible that you either reject it and therefore you have created a phobia, or you face it, previously suffering the panic that causes you to face speaking in front of an audience. This is despite the fact that there is nothing left of the child of that time in you. You may not even remember the name of the teacher, and may even have consciously forgotten that event. But your unconscious does not forget the program that one day was recorded in your mind: "Public speaking is dangerous."

However, that can be changed with NLP: This instrument allows us to become not only the one we could be if we took full advantage of our capabilities but also the one we want to be reinterpreting the information that comes from abroad. That is, giving it a different meaning than certain events that have marked us powerfully throughout our existence. NLP works with the specific sensory experience stored in the brain, and to work with it, it is necessary to find out the structure and the conditions under which that experience was processed and stored. From this knowledge, we can modify its influence on us to make it easier for us to achieve our goals.

Effective NLP therapy involves change.

The reality, as such, does not exist. Each person has his own reality, that is, human beings know reality through the interpretation that each of us makes of it. Throughout the history of humanity, many thinkers have referred to the undoubted difference between the world and our experience of it. From the illustrious Greek philosopher Zeno to an eminent German thinker like Schopenhauer and many other privileged brains throughout the history of thought. They have each insisted that human beings do not act directly in the world, but in the representation every one of us creates of it. That personal representation will determine our way of perceiving reality and the options that we may have at our disposal.

Based on our own experiences, the place we were born, the family that corresponds to us, the behavior of the people around us, and in general the experiences we face, we draw our own conclusions about the outside world. That is, we create a MAP of reality that will be different for each person. This MAP will constitute our guide to move through life and will absolutely condition our habitual behavior, shaping our lives and our relationships.

Neurolinguistic Programming (NLP), through its techniques and tools, allows us to know our MAP and that of others so that we can modify and even expand it in order to achieve the objectives we set for ourselves. An effective therapy implies, in some way, a change in the way in which the person represents his experience of the world.

NLP methodology: the modeling process

The methodology of NLP is modeling. Modeling consists of finding the essential components of the behavior to be reproduced, to achieve an equivalent result.

Modeling is a process that allows you to recreate successful behaviors. It is a process that consists of two phases:

The first is to carefully study the attitudes and behaviors of the subject to be modeled, to find out how he does what he does excellently.

The second is to transmit in a clear and understandable way the conclusions drawn from said observation. This is so that other people who have not participated in the observation are able, from the created model, to reproduce the original behavior that they want to learn, and obtain similar efficacy results.

To be able to model effectively, a series of specific skills are essential, such as:

Sensory acuity: It is necessary to have the senses in a position to appreciate any element; however insignificant it may seem. That is, open and trained to capture the information transmitted by the subject to be modeled.

Verbal and non-verbal skills to obtain high-quality information.

NLP is based on looking for the "how" more than the "why." The question "why" is aimed at finding out the causes that generated the problem and therefore is oriented towards the problem. Instead, the question "how" focuses on the way something is done and therefore is a generator of change. From the "how" perspective, one thing is done in one way. But it would also be possible to do it in another, making it susceptible to being modified.

A special attitude that implies being curious, placing yourself in a permanent state of resources, as well as passion and commitment to what you do, and a willingness to move towards change.

This could be summed up in three words that define the modeling process: CURIOSITY, EXPERIMENTATION, and FLEXIBILITY.

Well Bandler and Grinder, after a long time of detailed observation and after learning to model successful people, extrapolated it to people who wanted to introduce a change in their lives. They focused on discovering the process by which the person with whom they wanted to work, incorporated at a certain moment the information that caused them a certain vision of a situation. This was what later constituted their problem, (for example: "I will never have success," or "I am not able to do anything right "..."). From there they set out to help him "unlearn" what had previously been recorded in his brain. And to introduce into him a "new program" that would allow him to eliminate the old automatism of behavior or thought, as well as direct him in the direction of the objective that he wished to achieve.

The 10 NLPs (Neuro-linguistic Programming)

Concepts, Premises and theoretical bases on which NLP is based.

The NLP is a collection of approaches focused on recognizing and utilizing thinking patterns that affect a person's actions as a means of improving quality and solving problems.

Among other things, NLP's goals are to correct cognitive experiences, make them more efficient, and include a set of appropriate techniques and skills for the better adaptation to certain circumstances that occur in everyday life.

It is important to note that this method is not based on any hypothesis but instead is a collection of studies, analyses, and techniques. Therefore, it is important to test how it operates through its basic foundations, that is, the NLP principles.

After setting out the goals of Neurolinguistic Programming, we present below the NLP's ten principles:

1. The map to the inside is special

One of the NLP concepts refers to the orientation people have for them in the world. The person's way of orienting has to do with his inner map. The interior map is simple in the early stages of life. The map becomes more complicated as we grow, however, and new pathways are opened.

The more complete the map, the more alternatives the individual will have for success. The map of the world is individual, and it is created from our own experiences so that each person has his map, and there are no two maps the same.

2. The best map is the one which offers more than one path

The more detailed map is also more reliable as discussed in the previous stage and will provide more opportunities to achieve a goal or solve the problem. It has to do with versatility and being able to respond to a life event in different ways. The map is not the territory it represents, but it would have a similar layout to the territory and be more useful if it is accurate.

3. Every action has goodwill

This may be one of the NLP concepts that have been discussed the most. This argument refers to the fact that intrinsically every person, and every action has a positive purpose. For example, it can be that someone believes a smoker has a good intent to smoke. Yet, according to this theory, the smoker may smoke to relax or be accepted socially. NLP helps to redirect the positive intent into a more adaptive and effective behavioral pattern for the patient.

4. The Experience structure

This theory illustrates how a certain system is composed of experience. Every thinking, feeling, memory, or experience consists of a number of elements. This implies that if each experience has a structure, its impact can be modified thanks to a change in its composition.

5. There is one solution to all problems

This idea is that there is one solution to all problems. While it will seem utopian, certain ideas cannot be applied as often. Many times, issues can occur that don't have a simple solution. It has to do with the map. The individual has fewer solutions to the particular problem as the fewer roads or alternatives he has. Additionally, the definition of the problem is related to the map material. A richer map providing more services will consider certain conditions as less troublesome.

6. All have the power they need

This is one of the NLP's principles, which has to do with the person's personal growth, as it relates to the fact that each person has the strength required to accomplish what is proposed. The problem occurs when the restricted creeds of the individual impair self-confidence.

7. The mind and body are a part of the same mechanism

This definition applies to the body and mind of the human being. In other words, the body is influenced by every sensation and every emotion. That, in reverse, is also valid. A disease that affects the body, for example, will have psychological consequences. For NLP, therefore, it is important to change the thinking that modifies bodily problems. Did you hear about embodied cognition, by the way?

8. The importance of correspondence depends on the outcome

Clear communication guidelines need to be drawn up which do not give rise to misunderstandings, nor an opportunity for biased personal interpretations by the message recipient.

9. There are no mistakes but chances

If an individual is constantly on the move, he has various paths to attain the target. Failures must be seen as opportunities, that is, as steps that allow us to surmount and step in the direction we want.

10. If it doesn't work, you've got to try something new

People often believe that they do something that doesn't work, so they don't alter the way they behave. At this point, it makes sense to use the popular expression "do not expect different outcomes, if you still do the same thing." The NLP professionals strive to help identify and change certain counterproductive patterns that fall on the same stone over and over again.

CHAPTER 7

VERBAL VS. NON-VERBAL COMMUNICATION

Communication can vary based on how the information is passed on and how the recipient interprets it.

Communication can, therefore, be divided into two main groups: verbal and nonverbal symbols.

Visual contact is one where the meaning is verbalized, either verbally or in writing. Although non-verbal communication happens without using words, gestures, looks, body movements are used, among others.

These two forms of communication are frequently used concurrently when a message is sent, creating a mixed communication.

What is verbal communication?

It's the process of communicating with two or more people, exchanging knowledge through the word.

To clarify the meaning and offer a better understanding of what is said, verbal communication is also complemented by nonverbal communication. However, these two forms of communication can often contradict each other during the message's transmission.

Verbal communication involves using words to construct

sentences that convey ideas. Such words can be conveyed either orally or by writing.

Oral communication

It is one where words are spoken or sounds are made verbally. Intonation and vocalization play a vital role in this form of communication because the message arrives quickly, and the receiver may understand it.

This style of communication uses important elements, such as para-linguistics, which, while not being verbal, helps to show emotions and feelings when speaking. So, tones and sounds are emitted which, among others, indicate fear, surprise, interest or disinterest, or mischief.

Throughout history, oral communication has developed with the roots of languages and the linguistic characteristics of each population.

Definitions of oral communication may be a peer-to-peer call, a scream of surprise, or a phone chat.

Written communication

It is achieved using written codes. In comparison to oral communication, written communication can last over time. It means that the receptor interaction is not immediately occurring.

With the advent of modern media, written communication has evolved, and will still change as science and technology continue to generate new communication networks.

Examples of writing may be hieroglyphs, notes, e-mails, or chats.

What is non-verbal communication?

This is when non-linguistic signals are used to relay messages. It is the oldest form of communication since it was the way people interacted when there was no language in existence.

Nonverbal signals may be unwittingly transmitted when interpreted involuntarily.

Nonverbal communication may become unclear because it is not always possible to regulate what is communicated with the picture or body gestures. Likewise, several times, the reader does not view these signals in the right way.

For this purpose, nonverbal communication usually seeks to reinforce the message that is verbally conveyed. And the recipient can read the message easier.

Nonverbal signals can also be conveyed via written correspondence, for example, by using colors or emoticons.

Types of nonverbal communication may be movements, words, features of the face and body, attitude, voice, physical presence, or colors.

Types of verbal and non-verbal communication.

Verbal and nonverbal communication can be conveyed in various forms and for specific purposes. Taking into account these parameters, they can be categorized according to the relationship between the sender and the recipient of the means of communication used.

Based on the sender/recipient relationship

Unilateral

Is done when the recipient does not act as a sender as well. For instance: on traffic signs or advertisements.

Bilateral

It happens when the sender may become a recipient, too. It occurs in every informal interaction.

Depending on the communication medium

Audiovisual

It includes messages which are transmitted through conventional audiovisual media such as film, radio, and television.

Printed

Such forms of written correspondence include, among others, newspapers, magazines, brochures, posters, leaflets.

Digital

Thanks to technology, digital communication is possible; this includes emails, social networks such as Facebook or Instagram, and other channels that allow large dissemination of information such as YouTube, Podcast, or Blogspot.

Traditional media now also have a multimedia presence, both audiovisual and literary.

Differences between verbal and non-verbal communication

Our ancestors hunted and lived as a group where they depended on each other to feel safe, accompanied, and to survive. Our success as a species and as individuals depends upon our ability to communicate effectively. Communication is a natural phenomenon; it is an act of interaction in which we exchange knowledge with others. There are two different types of verbal and nonverbal contact.

Verbal and non-verbal communication form our business and interpersonal relationships with others, as well as our political, personal health, and physical and psychological well-being. The first step in enhancing communication is to consider the various dimensions of verbal and nonverbal communication, and the important roles they perform in our relationships with others.

Verbal communication: characteristics

Verbal communication is one in which the sender uses words, whether spoken or written, to convey the message to the receiver. It is the most effective form of communication because the exchange of information and feedback is very fast. There is less chance of misunderstanding since communication between the parties is clear; that is, the parties are using words to express what they want to say.

Communication can be done in two ways:

- Face-to-face interaction: oral, conferences, phone calls, seminars, etc.
- In writing: letters, emails, text messages, etc.

There are two main types of communication:

Formal communication, also called official communication: it is a type of communication in which the sender follows a predefined channel to transmit the information to the receiver.

Informal communication: it is the type of communication in which the sender does not follow any predefined channel to transmit the information.

Non-verbal communication: examples and types

Non-verbal communication is based on the understanding or interpretation of each of the parts that are part of the communicative act since the transmission of messages does not occur through words but through signs. Therefore, if the recipient fully understands the message, and adequate feedback occurs, the communication will be successful. A very clear example of this type of communication is facial expression, gestures, and body position when speaking.

In many situations, it complements verbal communication to obtain a more global vision of the situation, to understand the state of people (if they are nervous, relaxed, sad...) and certain personality characteristics (if the person is shy, outgoing...). Therefore, it serves to obtain that information that the speech does not provide us. The types of non-verbal communication are as follows:

Chromium: Is the use of time in communication. For example, punctual or untimely people, speed of a speech, etc.

Proxemic: Is the distance maintained by the person with others during the communicative act. Proxemic tells us when communication is intimate, personal, social, and public.

Vowel: The volume, tone, and timbre of voice used by the sender.

Haptic: Is the use of touch in communication that expresses emotions and feelings.

Kinesia: Is the study of the person's body language: gestures, postures, facial expressions...

Artifacts: It is the appearance of the person which shows aspects of their personality, for example, the way of dressing, jewelry, lifestyle, etc.

Verbal communication is a type of communication in which words are used to share information, whether in speech type or writing, with others. By contrast, non-verbal communication does not use words, but other modes of communication, such as body language, facial expressions, sign language, etc. are used. Here are some of the differences between verbal and nonverbal communication:

Verbal communication uses words, while non-verbal communication is based on signs.

There are fewer opportunities for confusion between the sender and receiver in verbal communication, whereas, in nonverbal communication, understanding is more difficult since language is not used.

In verbal communication, the exchange of messages is faster, which makes receiving feedback very fast. Nonverbal communication is based more on understanding, which takes time and is therefore slower.

In verbal communication, the presence of both parties in the place is not necessary, since it can also be done if the parties are in different places. On the other hand, in non-verbal communication, both parties must be there, at the time of communication.

In verbal communication, documentary evidence is maintained if the communication is formal or written. But there is no conclusive evidence of nonverbal communication.

Verbal communication fulfills the most natural human desire to speak. In the case of non-verbal communication, feelings, emotions, or personality are communicated through the acts performed by the parties in the communicative action.

It is important to comment that both types of communication complement each other, and, in many cases, they occur simultaneously.

CHAPTER 8

3 NLP TOOLS YOU SHOULD KNOW

Have you heard about NLP, but you are not very clear about how to apply it in your life or your business? Neurolinguistic Programming (NLP) has become one of the most important disciplines, especially when we want to achieve certain objectives.

This means that, when modifying our emotions, belief system, and way of communicating, we can change in the same way the reality and the image that we have of ourselves.

That is why we will show you 3 valuable tools of neurolinguistic programming, collected from the hands of experts so that they are useful to increase the well-being of your businesses and your life.

Anchors

Have you ever consciously or unconsciously suggested to yourself to change a negative sensation for a positive one? Then you have possibly applied what is known as anchoring.

Anchoring is the association between an external stimulus and positive behavior that you want to adopt. It is carried out by means of anchors such as words, perceptions, or gestures that transfer us to mental well-being.

The anchors come to act as the hinges of a door. Our environment is full of these anchors so that the brain takes advantage of them through its association mechanisms.

Reframing

Have you heard that to see things from a different point of view, you "turn the tables" or look for a new perspective on life? All these allegories and phrases belong to an NLP technique known as reframing.

It is a tool that allows us to change the frame of reference that we live to give it a different meaning, so that the emotional behavior that we initially adopted is replaced by a new one, and therefore more optimistic.

To guide us to reframing, some of the new motivational speakers motivate us to see the jar as partially filled and still not completely empty, to change the context of the picture to make it appear prettier, and to find unexplored points in situations that might seem adverse.

The swish pattern

Have you ever wanted to change behaviors that you don't like about yourself? If the answer is positive, it means that you are someone who wants to be a better person, and therefore the swish pattern technique is for you.

The swish pattern is a method of NLP that is applied to modify behaviors, which has the function of taking unwanted behaviors to transform them into desires to be someone you really want to be.

It is a tool that is helpful in changing unwanted behaviors and modes of perception.

The second projected image must produce a strong and positive stimulus, this by applying the swish effectively.

Importance of NLP tools

Perhaps what is most striking about the tools of neurolinguistic programming is that they are very effective. That is why this type of therapy is usually applied in a massive way today.

It should be noted that these three tools are not applied together in all cases. This means that everything will depend on the professional who moderates the behaviors and, on the stimulus, most related to the individual who must be moderate.

CHAPTER 9

BODY LANGUAGE

Many studies have been carried out in body language, and several hypotheses have been born, such as one where 93 percent of the contact is non-verbal.

However, body language is not a marginal impact on our social skills and an excellent indicator of our partners' real emotions.

You certainly know people who create suspicion, although not especially negative or neutral. You couldn't say what it is, but it gives you a feeling that you don't want to confess your true emotions.

This is because a contradiction exists between their verbal communication and their body language. You can even generate this contradiction yourself without knowing it!

And others radiate great charisma, on the other hand, without being particularly talkative. Your body is aligned with your language of the word, and it conveys warmth and trust.

What is body language?

Body-language is a communication process utilizing the movements and postures of the body and its expression to convey information on the feelings and thoughts of the sender.

This is typically performed on an undisclosed stage, and therefore often is a direct indication of the emotional condition of the individual. This is part of non-verbal communication, along with vocal intonation.

Body language cannot always be interpreted correctly because it can be affected by various environmental factors. The definition of a particular physical sign can never be concluded; it is necessary to look at consistent signs and to eliminate possible external causes (temperature, noise, fatigue, etc.).

The keys to body language

1. The face is the loudspeaker of emotions

Therefore, it is claimed to be a soul representation. However, as in any non-verbal language interpretation, you must be careful not to measure facial expressions individually because they typically form part of a global emotional state and can lead to various interpretations.

Is it not true that when a child sees anything he doesn't like he covers his eyes in a bid to get it out of his reality? Or do you hide after you say a lie by covering your mouth?

Though the magnitude of adults is significantly lower, we are still, to some degree, connected with this primitive behavior. And that provides a lot of hints because there is also a lot of unconscious attempts to mask what we say, hear or see in the face.

In general, it is often the product of some negative thought, such as insecurities, or distrust, when someone puts his hands on his face. Several unique examples are given here.

Covering or rubbing your mouth: If you do it, you might try to cover something. It may be an indication that someone thinks something is concealed from him as he listens.

Touching the ear: It reflects the unconscious desire to block the words. When your speaker does that during the discussion, he might want you to stop talking.

Nose touch: Might mean somebody's lying. Catecholamines, which inflame the inner tissues of the nose and can cause itching, are released when you lie. It also occurs if someone is irritated or angry.

Rubbing an eye: This is an attempt to hide what you see to avoid looking at the person to whom you are lying. Caution people who brush and rub their eyes a lot when they talk to you.

Scratching your neck: It's a sign of confusion or skepticism about what you say.

To put a finger or something to the mouth: It means insecurity or the need to calm down, in an unconscious expression of returning to the safety of the mother.

2. Head positions

Understanding the meaning of the different situations that someone can take with their heads is very important in realizing their real intentions, such as the desire to like, cooperate, or be arrogant.

Pay special attention to very exaggerated postures, because they mean that this person is doing it consciously to influence you.

Raising your head and projecting your chin forward: A sign that purports to communicate aggressiveness and power expressly.

Nodding: It is a social expression that can spread positive feelings. It communicates engagement and consent, but it can communicate that enough has been learned if it is done many times quickly.

Tilting your head: A gesture of submission by showing your throat. You will raise your interlocutor's trust in you if you do it as you nod while listening to others. For women, it was also seen as an interest in a man.

Helping up the face with your hands: The face is normally revealed to the interlocutor to be "presented." It indicates the other person's attraction.

Resting the head on the hand: It is a sign of approval if the palm is closed. This can indicate boredom or lack of interest if the palm is open.

3. Eye contact has a lot to do with the pupil's dilation or contraction that responds to the inner states.

That is why light eyes seem to be more attractive than dark eyes: because they allow for a more easily noticeable dilated response from the pupil, which is related to positive emotions.

As you talk, between 40 and 60% of the time, you usually maintain eye contact. That's how your brain tries to gain access to information (NLP postulates that you can look sideways, depending on the type of information you're searching for, although that has been clinically proven not to be true).

A lack of eye contact can be seen as nervousness or shyness in certain social settings. So just hesitating before answering saves you the time you need to access details without looking away.

If you make a case, looking squarely in the eyes is always helpful to strengthen your conviction. Yet other functions of the gaze are also available.

The size of the pupils may vary: not controllable, but with the presence of increased pupils, something positive is typically seen.

In any case, they are very subtle changes that are often obscured by low-intensity environmental changes. In the effort to synchronize body language and establish a broader link, the mirror neurons are also found to be responsible for changing our pupils' size to that of our interlocutor.

Raising your eyebrows: it is a social welcome that means a lack of apprehension and trust.

Lower your head and lookup: This is a role that transmits sensuality to men seen in the female sex. Many profile images of women shot from above (sometimes for additional purposes to display cleavage) are seen on online dating sites. For men, the reverse is true: lower shots tend to be bigger and more powerful.

Maintaining the gaze: for women, the eye contact may be a sign of the sexual desire for 2 or 3 seconds and look down. Many ways to block the view of a person who stands before you out of boredom or distrust: this is another way.

Sideways looking: a way to convey frustration, because you want to avoid routes unconsciously.

4. Smile Types

The smile is an endless source of sense and feeling. You can have a full chapter about all the advantages of the smile and what can be communicated with it. Smiling is also an extremely contagious act, thanks to mirror neurons, that can cause very positive feelings in other people.

Moreover, a vast number of smile types can be differentiated from what they communicate. For instance, the left side of the mouth appears to grow higher in a false smile since the most professional part of the brain is the right hemisphere, which mostly regulates the rest of the body.

The natural smile is the one that causes the eyes to wrinkle and raise the cheeks and the eyebrows a little.

A closed smile with clenched lips denotes that one does not want to exchange emotions with you and this is a strong sign of refusal.

The biological function of a smile is to create a social connection through the fostering of confidence and the elimination of any threat. It has also been shown that submissions are transmitted. Those who want to give up power and women who want their influence in the predominantly male professional atmosphere avoid smiling.

5. Position of the arms

The arms, along with the hands, support the majority of the movements you make. They also allow defending the most vulnerable areas of your body in situations of perceived insecurity.

The proprioception has taught us that the direction of contact between the mind and the body is mutually reciprocal. Your body expresses it unconsciously whenever you feel an emotion. The reverse happens: if you knowingly take a role, the subconscious will sense the emotion. This is especially evident when you cross your arms.

Many people think they are crossing their arms because they feel more relaxed. Yet movements appear normal if they are in line with the person's behavior, and science has shown, however comfortable a move, that crossing them can predispose to a critical attitude. Remember that you don't cross your arms when you have a nice time with friends!

That is what you express when your weapons assume a particular position: cross your arms, disagree, and deny. In a sensual sense, women typically do so when men who look too offensive or too unattractive are in front of them.

Crossing one arm in front to hold the other arm: denotes a lack of self-confidence when needing to feel hugged.

Arms crossed with thumbs-up: defensive posture, but at the same time, it wants to convey pride.

Place your hands in front of your genitalia: in people, it gives you a sense of protection when you feel sensitivity.

Confidence and fearlessness are demonstrated by exposure to weak points such as the chest, neck, and groin. In circumstances of uncertainty, it may be helpful to take the approach to try to build trust.

Usually speaking, folding your arms means fear. This is why the body must be secured. The watch can be changed, the case is put in front of the body of the bag with both hands before the arm, but they both mean the same thing.

6. Hand gestures

Hands and arms are a moving part of the body and thus provide a wide variety of non-verbal contact possibilities. The most popular one is to use them to display dominance or sexuality in some parts of the body.

They are also intended to help and reinforce verbal messages.

The brain, named the Broca region, is part of the speech cycle. However, the fact that it is triggered by moving your hands has been confirmed. It means that gesturing is directly related to expression, and it can also boost your verbal capacity when expressing yourself. Very useful for people who get stuck in public speaking!

A research found that reinforcing a sentence with gestures earlier helps the words you use to come to mind, and also that the message is much more compelling and understandable. Through this study, it was found that verbal signification, such as pointing back about the past, are the most persuasive gestures.

Below is all that is understood on the importance of hand gestures:

- **Shows open palm:** Expresses sincerity and honesty, while closing the fist shows the opposite.

- **Hands in Pockets:** This indicates patriotism and lack of interaction or circumstance participation.

- **Emphasize something with the hand:** Generally, when someone gives two points of view with the hands, the one they like best is emphasized with the dominant hand and palm up.

- **The fingers on both hands are interlaced:** Transmits a repressed, nervous, or pessimistic disposition. If your interlocutor takes that stance, split it by offering him something, so he has to keep it.

- **Fingertips together:** Communicates confidence and security, but arrogance can be mistaken. Quite useful for detecting whether opponents play poker with good hands.

- **Holding the other hand behind your back:** This is an attempt to restrain yourself; therefore, it shows anger or an effort to mask nervousness.

- **Showing thumbs out of pockets:** In men, it represents an attempt to demonstrate confidence and authority in front of women who attract them. But it may also be a way to communicate aggressiveness in a conflictual situation.

- **Just conceal the thumbs in the pockets**: It's a pose that frames and shows the genital region, and is, therefore, a sexually open approach by men to a woman who lacks fear or sex.

- **Place your hands on your hips:** Suggests a subtly threatening stance as you want your physical presence to be increased. Many people use it for both establishing dominance in their social circle and becoming more masculine in the presence of those women who attract them. The more open the face, the more violent sub-communications it will render.

7. Leg position

In body language, the legs play an exciting role. As our rational mind is farther away from the central nervous system (the brain), it has less power over them and helps them to communicate inner emotions more openly.

The farther a portion of the body is separated from the brain, the less influence you have of what it is doing.

The human being is usually conditioned to get back to what he wants and away from what he doesn't want. How someone puts their legs will give you some of the most useful hints about nonverbal communication because it will take you to where they want to go.

The front foot: Almost always the most advanced foot points to where you want to go. It also often points to the person you find most fascinating or desirable in a social situation with many people.

If you want someone to feel like you're giving them your full attention emotionally, make sure your feet face them. Similarly, when your interlocutor points his feet to the door rather than to you, it is a pretty clear indication that he wants to end the discussion.

Crossed legs: A defensive and closed posture that safeguards the genitals. This should express women's sexual rejection of men in the form of courtship.

Getting a person sitting in a social situation with their arms and legs crossed probably means they've withdrawn from the conversation. Researchers Allan and Barbara Pease performed an experiment that found that if they listened with their arms and legs crossed, people recalled less information from a meeting.

Sitting with one leg elevated resting on the other: Typically masculine, reveals a competitive or ready to argue attitude; it would be the seated display version of the crotch.

Widely separated legs: Another masculine gesture that wants to convey dominance and territoriality.

Sitting with curled legs: In women, it usually means some shyness and introversion.

Sitting parallel with one leg on top of the other: Some scholars agree that in women, when attempting to attract attention to the legs, it can be perceived as courtship, as they are more pressed in this pose. They have a more sensual, youthful look.

It can be very helpful for you to learn to spot differences between verbal and body language. What the body shows is generally very accurate, as humans cannot monitor all the signals it emits.

Note that all of these bodily signals must be viewed in a global sense and with some limitations. Do not bring a single expression to a close. Someone could cross his arms because he's just cold, or because it's a trend that has mechanized and lost some of its real sense.

The superpowers of body language

The Little Mermaid

If superheroes, villains, and other cartoon characters have taught us anything, it's that with our bodies, we can transmit many things.

Contrary to popular belief, we are all experts in body language, as we know how to read, use, and decode its messages. Think about if your partner transforms into the Hulk, and you put a kitty face on him to calm him down. But what very few of us do is use it consciously to enjoy its benefits. Do you want to convey security, confidence, and power? Look at 5, not at all fancy body language recommendations inspired by cartoons:

Accurate and marked movements - any movement of the body is done with security and strength; always forward.

Open posture - the arms grasped in front, behind or crossed close the communication channels and communicate insecurity. Take the posture of Darth Vader or Wonder Woman from hands to waist to show tightness and dynamism, but with authority and power.

Smile - Peter Pan, in addition to following the first two recommendations, also smiles! That gives him a halo of confidence and security in everything he does. Imitate it!

Eye contact - Have you noticed that all cartoons have particularly large eyes? This is to give them a higher capacity for expression. Use your eyes to communicate what you want and to see beyond the obvious.

Sound voice - People associate powerful voices with confidence and authority. But don't be confused, don't scream or speak loudly, just make yourself heard clearly ... like Mufasa.

But the real superpower of body language is not only in the way they will perceive us and in what we will make others feel. The universities of Harvard and Berkeley have already verified that by creating these movements, our body will also feel power, confidence, and security, affecting our behavior and making us more productive.

Deception Spectrum

The first step that we are going to take to know the meaning of the word deceit is to proceed to discover its etymological origin. In doing so, we will find the fact that it emanates from Latin, and more exactly from the verb "ingannare", which is equivalent to "entangle someone or make fun of him."

Deception is the action and effect of misleading (to induce someone to believe what is not, give the appearance of truth, lie, produce illusion). For example:

"Mario could not bear the deception of his wife and left the city," "This financial operation has been the greatest deception to the Argentine people," "It is not magic, it is simple deception."

A deception, therefore, supposes a lack of truth in what is said, done, or thought. It is possible to link it with lies, cheating, or tricks. Some tricks try to protect the deceived (to prevent them from coming into contact with a painful reality) or provide fun (such as a joke or a magic trick).

Within personal relationships, and more precisely within romantic relationships, the most common deception is the one that hides infidelity. In this way, the infidel has sexual encounters with a third person while his official partner is unaware of this circumstance.

Inventing work meetings or professional trips are some of the tools that those who cheat on their boy or girl with another third person usually use. However, as a general rule, all this is generally discovered in the end, and most often, a breakup occurs.

Adults often trick children into developing games or keeping a fantasy. A typical deception is to spread the existence of Santa Claus as the person in charge of Christmas gifts. Parents often cheat on their children and claim that Santa Claus enters homes to drop gifts.

When a trick is to obtain a financial return, it is called a scam. This is a crime against patrimony or property: the scammer deceives the victim and makes him deliver a patrimonial asset by making him believe the existence of something non-existent. An example of a scam occurs when a person requests a cash advance as the first step in purchasing a car. The scammer claims that, with that first payment, you can start the process and buy the car. However, the vehicle will never be delivered, and the scammer keeps that money.

We would have to emphasize that in the bullfighting world, the term deception is also used, but with a meaning that has nothing to do with those exposed so far. Specifically, in this area, that word is used to refer to the crutch that the bullfighter uses to deceive the bull in front of him.

Deception is the action and effect of deceiving someone or deceiving themselves with some situation that happens. "I don't know why I am deceiving myself by continuing this relationship." "For me, the contest is purely and simply a hoax."

On the other hand, the lack of truth that something has or directly the falsity of something is called deception.

Basically, in deception, there is a total absence of truth in what is done, thought, or said. In general, cheating is associated with tricks. Tricks, with which the purpose of losing the truth is achieved without the person being able to perceive directly and clearly.

It should be noted then that normally the person to whom the deception is directed is especially guided by the deceiver, the person who specifies the deception, to fall for a lie. Now, such an action can be done to exercise evil, or conversely, someone can be tricked into avoiding suffering with the knowledge of any situation.

On the other hand, it is common to be deceived with a humorous motivation or in those cases in which it is addressed to a child, to involve the child in a special reality or situation. One of the most common deceptions in which children participate is instilling beliefs such as the existence of Santa Claus, the Three Kings, the Pérez mouse, among others.

CHAPTER 10

DEFINITION OF HYPNOSIS

Hypnosis, which comes from a Greek term meaning "numb," refers to the state or condition generated by hypnotism. This, in turn, is a procedure that involves inducing a person to drowsiness.

For example: "The mentalist subjected a man to hypnosis and made him crow like a chicken," "I don't believe in hypnosis," "The police in the last century used to resort to hypnosis for suspects, to tell the truth in their statements."

Hypnosis is said to be a physiological condition that causes a person to be able to act unconsciously, as ordered by the hypnotist. It should be clarified, however, that the results obtained in each case depend largely on the predisposition of the individuals.

Given its questionable use in magic shows and mentalism, the general perception of hypnotism does not position it as a serious topic, much less as a science. Often considered a sub-science, there are numerous books, both instructive and historicist, that address this phenomenon that raises countless questions, even the most skeptical. Once again, these sources are not entirely reliable, given the media and sensational nature of hypnotism in society.

Differences with autosuggestion

Also known as autohypnotism, it is associated with the repetition of acts or phrases to modify the mind itself. The mechanism is to make an idea part of our unconscious, of our conception of reality. Similarities can be identified, but auto-suggestion can also be an unconscious mechanism leading to self-destruction, whether it is used to stop smoking or remove bad behaviors. We find clear examples in people who despise themselves, who do not accept their bodies, who think they are unpleasant for others, either because of their physique or their personality. These individuals tell themselves over and over that they are worthless, that they are undesirable, and end up believing their words.

Hypnosis, Therapy and Neurolinguistic Programming

Outside of circuses and theaters, hypnosis has proven to be very effective in treatments against smoking, phobias of all kinds, obesity, as well as to combat pain, stimulate attention and improve memory. Often in no more than a couple of sessions, this procedure can uproot fears and feelings of rejection that make a person's life difficult. Also, altering the perception of a physical stimulus that used to be associated with great pain, making it more bearable by the individual.

And here, we come across a very popular concept since the 1970s: NLP or Neuro-linguistic Programming. This arises from the work of Richard Bandler (computer scientist) and John Grinder (psychologist and linguist) and describes the possibility of changing the brain's perception of reality, consequently altering its reaction to different stimuli and situations. If we take into account that each person sees the world in a particular way, we understand why certain phrases are funny for some and boring for others, as well as, on a deeper level, certain images go unnoticed by some but emotionally block others.

NLP can act on trauma, causing the patient to relive memories, reinterpret them with their unfailingly more mature mind, and restore them. According to studies, it is currently impossible to erase a portion of memory. This is the only way, discovered so far, to help those people living tormented by a horrible past, which they would discard if they had the opportunity.

Also, this type of therapy achieves very positive results to reinforce self-confidence. It is often applied to patients with self-esteem problems, offering them a much more positive vision of themselves and demonstrating, or allowing them to discover, those virtues that have been relegated for years.

Theories about hypnosis

Hypnosis is the subject of a variety of separate and contradictory hypotheses, some of which concentrate on brain function and others on the nature of the condition. Furthermore, there is a clear division between those who believe that consciousness prevails during the state of hypnotism and those who deny it flatly.

The five forms of hypnosis and their operating conditions

There is no one way to hypnotize. We show you the different forms that this technique can take.

Hypnosis is a technique that facilitates behavioral changes through suggestion. Depending on the term we use, we may classify hypnosis as a psychological disorder or a sequence of mental behaviors and processes; today, it is correlated with beliefs or brain waves by the medical community.

Throughout this section, we will look at the five most popular forms of hypnosis: the standard approach centered upon direct oral instructions, cognitive-compartmental hypnosis, self-hypnosis, neurology, and programming or NLP.

The five most popular types of hypnosis

Here are 5 of the best-known methods, including the use of hypnosis. There are, of course, many other variants, and practitioners or instruments can combine more than one form.

1) **Modern hypnosis (by suggestion)**

   The origin of mainstream hypnosis goes back to the unusual methods used by Franz Mesmer in magnets and popularized at the end of the 18th century. Earlier, James Braid expressed his resistance to the theory of the mesmeric system and proposed the hypnosis to be a nervous system condition.

   The typical hypnosis is based on the induction of a trance state. When the hypnotized person enters the trance state, his actions and mental contents are indicated in verbal form. Thus, the objective of this method is to influence behavior, for example, by suggesting that the person abandon a negative habit or belief.

   Today the classical method is still the most widely used form of hypnosis worldwide. It is theoretical in terms of the theory of Freud's unconscious mind, which, in addition to shaping guidelines so different from cognitivism, has characterized the later developments in psychoanalysis critically.

2) **Ericksonian hypnosis**

   This form of hypnosis is a product of a pioneer in this area and psychotherapy in general, an American psychologist, Milton H. Erickson. This author shouldn't be confused with Erik Erikson, a German evolutionary psychologist who is best known for his eight-stage psychosocial theory.

   Ericksonian hypnosis is not achieved by straightforward instructions, but by metaphors that encourage creativity and contemplation. Because of this, it is attributed to greater effectiveness than classic hypnosis in people who are refractory to hypnosis, with low suggestibility or who are skeptical about the procedure.

Erickson's influence is not limited to hypnosis and neurolinguistic programming, which we will discuss later. The strategic school and the quick therapy focused on approaches, both parts of the systematic approach took on the core feature of its intervention model, the weight of the interaction between the therapist and the client for achieving change.

3) Cognitive-computer hypnosis

The cognitive-computing viewpoint views hypnosis as a series of approaches that facilitate behavioral improvements through recommendations. The relationship between variables such as physical rest, the use of imagination, or the individual's desires and values is a result of this phenomenon.

Those clinicians who adhere to cognitive behavioral therapy use strategies for hypnosis to supplement broader procedures. It was extended in this context to issues as diverse as sleep-wake cycle disorders, psychiatric, drug-related disorders or post-traumatic stress disorders (in particular, tobacco).

4) Self-hypnosis

We speak of self-hypnosis when a person induces himself in this state through autosuggestion. Instruments that serve as supports are often used; the most popular are sound recordings, but tools that modify brain waves to alter the level of consciousness are also available.

This form of hypnosis is primarily used for non-particularly severe everyday difficulties. Therefore, for example, intrapersonal and interpersonal skills (such as stressfulness), stress management, and relaxation can be created, the scenario can be met, weight loss, and smoking can stop.

5) Neurolinguistic programming (NLP)

While it's not a hypnotic thing to say, the neural conditioning is closely related to these approaches (usually referred to as "NLP"). This method was developed for psychologically enhancing skills by Richard Bandler and John Grinder using "pension models."

The Milton Model is based on the hypnosis method developed by Milton Erickson; in this variant of NLP, the suggestion is practiced through metaphors. The use made by Bandler and Grinder in the Ericksonian hypnosis was, however, criticized for altering or under-viewing many of their fundamental ideas.

Neurological programming is known by the scientific community as pseudo-science and, therefore, as a fraud. His theories do not base themselves on an empirical framework, even though it does incorporate abstract concepts to give "theory" an air of legitimacy.

Myths of Hypnosis

The myths in hypnosis come from several centuries ago, either due to misinterpretations or unfounded beliefs, and that may condition us not to grasp the fundamental concepts of the practice of hypnosis.

With this, we try to normalize the most common hypnosis myths that usually affect the understanding and acceptance of this technique as a therapeutic tool.

Myth 1: The hypnotized subject is highly suggestible and can do whatever the hypnotist instructs

The suggestion is a part of the hypnotic process, which is reached after the induction phase. This phase can be accessed in very different ways: by an object attributed to a hypnogenic power like a clock, or by a suggestive mimicry. Or, by a simple blow of effect like a clap followed by the word "dream" that causes an interruption in the hypnotizable individual and causes him to enter a trance state.

The suggestion does not even require the presence of the suggestion, as it happens in the cases of autosuggestion, or the hypnotization at a distance using a recording or using the telephone.

It is in the suggestion phase the hypnotized are given a series of "suggestions," as their name suggests, so that they do, feel or perceive what the hypnotist tells them.

But in no case can suggestion make the subject do things contrary to his ethical code or contrary to the laws of nature. You cannot get a person to fly or override the law of gravity, nor can they lift a weight for which they are not physically prepared to bear.

Most often, the suggestions influence aspects that we are not consciously able to influence, such as digestion, respiration, body temperature. And also on the mind, enhancing psychic factors such as imagination, sensory perception, or increasing memory.

They can indeed be accomplished with suggestions that a person sees where there is no or stops seeing where there is. This is what we call positive or negative hallucinations, which revert once the suggestion is annulled and are nothing more than natural phenomena of increased imagination.

We do need to differentiate between the INTRAHIPNÓTICAS SUGGESTIONS, that is, those occurring during the hypnotic trance, and the POSTHIPNÓTICAS, those occurring under an intrahepatic order, after leaving the trance and before the effect of a particular trigger.

For example: "When you wake up, you will feel very calm, and that tranquility you will take with you every day until the next session. And every time you bring a glass of water to your mouth, you will realize that you are doing something very important for yourself ... The contact of the water with your lips will remind you that every time you drink, you are bringing something very necessary to you... The fact of drinking water makes you feel that you are moving towards your desired state, feeling more and more relaxed and at ease with yourself. "

Myth 2: Hypnosis achieves little less than magical results in the hypnotized

The conviction that is also very popular is that hypnosis is quite convenient, simple, successful therapy that needs no effort on the part of the consumer to change their behavior.

Hypnosis is a technique that makes the result of an operation simpler, rather than a treatment itself. Like other ways of using suggestion, it can speed up treatment, decreasing the person's subjective effort. However, the patient must be actively involved in the treatment to obtain the desired benefits.

Hypnosis is only one of the many working tools that the psychologist or doctor can use within the therapeutic context if he sees fit. Hypnosis does not "cure" anything of its own, and no one can hypnotize what they are not prepared to do without hypnosis.

For this reason, hypnosis can only be applied with guarantees, a professional duly qualified and trained for what he intends to solve, and provided that he is expressly qualified, also, to apply the hypnotic techniques of his patients.

Myth 3: Under the hypnotic state, you can access past lives or contact deceased people

The extraordinary hypnotic phenomena, the revival of past experiences, and other unusual events that are sometimes described as occurring under a hypnotic state have not been proven by science. Before them, we must keep a certain reserve, at least.

Recalling past lives, speaking unknown languages, or other intra-hypnotic paranormal phenomena, but without dismissing the likelihood that they could have happened in certain cases, is not an easy thing to do daily. There is still much to be discovered about its origin before concluding with adequate empirical validity.

Myth 4: The person who goes into a deep trance does not remember anything later

Amnesia may indeed occur on certain occasions during the trance, either under the hypnotist's command or spontaneously.

It is not regularly occurring in any case unless you access forgotten traumatic memories and choose to leave this field inaccessible from the consciousness in the benefit of the individual.

If it is very frequent, however, a temporal distortion occurs, since the subject during the trance has the perception that much less time passes than what happens in reality.

So, when you finish the trance process, open your eyes and look at the clock. You will have the feeling that much more time has passed than you thought: this is a characteristic of the trance state.

Myth 5: The hypnotized may remain forever in a hypnotic state

One of the most widespread myths is the fear of not being able to wake up, which we discussed earlier. This is something unfounded since the only thing that can happen, and, can quickly occur, is that the hypnotized person enters a physiological dream, from which you will wake up in the same way that you wake up every morning after the night's sleep.

What is Hypnotherapy?

Hypnosis or Hypnotherapy is a type of psychotherapy that uses guided methods of relaxation and intense concentration, focusing the client's attention to achieve a high state of consciousness that is sometimes called a trance. The person's attention is so concentrated that while in this state, everything that happens around him is temporarily blocked or ignored by the person who is in the hypnotic trance. An individual with the aid of a qualified therapist can focus their attention on certain thoughts or duties in this natural state.

How does hypnosis function?

The hypnotic state helps people to examine negative thoughts, emotions, and experiences that may have been shielded from their conscious minds. As an aid for psychotherapy in general, hypnosis can be used. Hypnosis can also encourage people to perceive other things differently, such as suppressing pain perception.

Hypnosis can be used as a treatment or medical diagnosis in two ways.

The most important risk is the likelihood of having false remembrances and becoming less successful than other, more proven, conventional psychiatric therapies.

Analysis: This approach uses a state of relaxation to investigate a potential psychological root cause of disease and symptoms, including an incident of trauma that a person has unconsciously suppressed. The pain can be dealt with in psychotherapy until it is known.

Which occurs in a session of hypnotherapy?

The therapist's initial task is to establish a good

relationship with the client. This involves encouraging the client to talk about their concerns. The therapist may spend time with him first to conduct a medical history. As well as establishing a medical history, the examination helps to build trust between the therapist and the client. Feeling safe and comfortable with the therapist helps induce a hypnotic trance.

The goals for therapy are discussed and agreed between the two, and a full explanation of what Hypnosis consists of is provided. Any questions or misconceptions about hypnosis are also addressed.

A trance state is possible in several different ways. The therapist talks in a quiet, gentle voice and generally sits on a chair or a recliner. You may be asked to imagine or visualize yourself walking down a path, or you may be made to look at a fixed point, or simply hear the sound of the therapist's voice. To deepen the trance, the therapist can count from 10 to 1 or ask you to imagine walking down a flight of stairs. You will then feel very relaxed, but aware of your surroundings.

The duration of treatments depends on the problem or symptoms and individual circumstances. With some people, a problem like nail-biting can be successfully treated in one sitting. Other problems, like panic attacks, can take up to 5 or 6 sessions.

During therapy, clients are taught to induce self-hypnosis as part of a series of therapeutic home tasks.

It normally takes 1 ½ hours to start the first session and then 1 ½ hours after.

Things you should know about hypnosis:

- One can still be hypnotized against their will as they always track all the feedback, even though they are hypnotized.
- The entire aim of clinical hypnosis is to restore the lost control, and hence the symptom or problem has been induced.
- Approximately 85% of people of all ages are expected to respond easily to hypnosis.

How is Hypnosis beneficial?

The hypnotic state allows an individual to have more discussion and proposals. For several illnesses, it may improve many therapies, including:

- Phobias, fears, and anxiety
- Sleep disorders
- Depression
- Stress
- Post-traumatic stress
- The pain of loss

Hypnosis can also be used to relieve discomfort and resolve problems such as smoking or unhealthy consumption. This may also be effective for those with serious symptoms who need to tackle emergencies.

What are the disadvantages of Hypnosis?

The case of a person with psychotic symptoms, such as hallucinations and delusions, or anyone who uses narcotics or alcohol, cannot be suitable for hypnosis. It can only be used to manage pain after a doctor has examined the individual for any physical condition that needs medication or surgery. Hypnosis may also be a less effective form of therapy than other psychiatric disorders.

Some therapists use Hypnosis to retrieve repressed memories, which they possibly believe are linked to a person's mental disorder. Hypnosis, however, often poses a risk of false impressions, usually as a result of the therapist's unwanted suggestions. That's why the use of hypnosis is still controversial with many mental illnesses, including dissociative disorders.

Is it risky to get hypnosis?

No negative technique is hypnosis. It is not controlling or brainwashing, as was often claimed. A therapist cannot make a person uncomfortable or unable to do something. The most significant danger is that false remembrances would be less likely than other traditional psychological therapies that have proved to be more effective.

CHAPTER 11

WHAT IS BRAINWASHING?

The concept of "brainwashing" is very close to that of "mind control." It is an idea without a strictly scientific basis. It proposes that the will, thoughts and other mental facts of individuals can be modified through persuasion techniques, with which unwanted ideas would be introduced into the psyche of a "victim."

If we define the concept in this way, we see that it bears a marked similarity with another more typical of the vocabulary of psychology: that of suggestion, which refers to the influence that some individuals can exert on the mental contents of others (or on the own, in which case we speak of autosuggestion). However, the term "suggestion" is less ambitious.

Although the idea of brainwashing is not entirely incorrect, this popular concept has unscientific connotations that have led many experts to reject it in favor of more modest ones. The instrumental use of the term in legal proceedings has contributed to this, especially in disputes over child custody.

Brainwashing examples

It is common for complex phenomena such as suicide or terrorism to be explained by many people through the concept of brainwashing, especially in cases in which the subjects are seen as young and influential people. Something similar applies to sects, religions, conduct during wars, or radical political ideologies.

Concerning the latter case, it is worth mentioning that brainwashing has been used above all in attempts to give a simple explanation to events related to violence. Events such as the massacres that occurred in the context of Nazism and other types of totalitarianism.

Subliminal advertising is another fact that we can relate to the idea of brainwashing. This type of promotion, which is prohibited in countries like the United Kingdom, consists of the inclusion of messages that do not reach the threshold of consciousness but are automatically perceived.

Moreover, psychology itself has often been accused of being a brainwashing method. Particularly well-known is the case of Pavlov and Skinner's behaviorism, criticized by other experts and in works such as "The Clockwork Orange." Psychoanalysis and techniques such as cognitive restructuring have received similar signs of rejection.

History and popularization of the concept

The concept of brainwashing first emerged in China to describe the Chinese Communist Party's persuasion of opponents of the Maoist government. The term "xinao," which literally translates as "brainwash," was a play on words that referred to the cleansing of the mind and body promoted by Taoism.

In the 1950s, the term was adopted and applied by the United States Army and Government to justify the fact that some American prisoners had collaborated with their captors during the Korean War. It has been argued that their objective may have been to limit the public impact of the revelation that chemical weapons had been used.

Later Russian historian Daniel Romanovsky claimed that the Nazis had used brainwashing techniques (including re-education programs and mass propaganda) to promote their ideas among the population of Belarus. In particular, the conception of the Jews as an inferior race.

However, the popularization of brainwashing is primarily due to popular culture. Before "The Clockwork Orange" appeared the novel "1984" by George Orwell, in which a totalitarian government manipulates the population through lies and coercion. Sauron's mind control in "The Lord of the Rings" has also been associated with brainwashing.

View from psychology

Psychology generally understands the phenomena attributed to brainwashing through more operative and more limited concepts, such as persuasion and suggestion, which includes hypnosis. In these cases, changes in behavior depend largely on the subject's autosuggestion from external stimuli.

In 1983 the American Psychological Association, the hegemonic body in the field of psychology, commissioned clinical psychologist Margaret Singer to lead a working group to investigate the phenomenon of brainwashing. However, they accused Singer of presenting biased data and speculation, and the project was canceled.

It cannot be stated categorically that brainwashing exists as an independent phenomenon due to the ambiguity of its formulation. In any case, many authors defend that the use of powerful persuasion techniques is evident in contexts such as the media and advertising; however, it is advisable to avoid such topics.

Social influence happens when a person is influenced by feelings, beliefs or behaviors. In other ways, social power can be seen in reverence, socialization, peer pressure, loyalty, leadership, persuasion, marketing and sales. In 1958, psychologist Herbert Kelman described three different methods of shaping society.

Social influence

In the face of a persuasive message, the recipient can:

- Process the message rationally.

- Let yourself be carried away by heuristics.

For some authors such as Allport, social influence is the central object of study in Social Psychology. Allport defines the study of social influence: I try to understand and explain the way in which the thoughts, feelings, and behaviors of individuals are influenced by the real, imagined, or implicit presence of others. People intervene, sometimes as an influential agent, sometimes as a target that is influenced by other human beings. Influence is not always deliberate or explicit.

Intended social influence or persuasion

Through the processes of influence and persuasion, our affections, beliefs, attitudes, intentions, and behaviors are configured. The intention to influence is always aimed at achieving a change in the behavior of others, individuals, or groups. Sometimes the objective is to achieve a specific behavior (that they prepare breakfast for us); other times, it is intended to influence attitudes (announcement of nature). Attempts to influence can occur in face-to-face processes.

CHAPTER 12

SOCIAL INFLUENCE

Social influence occurs when emotions, opinions, or behaviors are affected by another person. Although it may seem that it is not very common, since most of the people with whom we deal are not going to try to change our attitudes, social influence occurs continuously in our lives.

From the moment we enter a supermarket, the vendors are going to offer us discounted products. The mechanic is going to advise us on a tire change when we only want to check the car oil. Friends are going to tell us which music is the best. Our partner will advise us on our wardrobe. Thus, in a large number of situations, others will try to influence us almost without us noticing.

First contributions to social influence

Social influence has been a major topic in social psychology. In the past, social influence has been used to explain acts as horrifying as those committed by the Nazis. It has also served to explain the behaviors of traitors who abandoned their side to fight with the opposite side.

To reach these conclusions, many experiments were carried out. Among them, three stand out for the revolution they supposed at the time. These experiments broke with preconceived beliefs, and their results were hardly assumable. These experiments were as follows:

Cialdini's experiments

One of the most famous researchers in this field is Robert Cialdini. Working as a car salesman, Cialdini discovered six factors of social influence that he called the "weapons of influence" (Cialdini, 2001). These factors are the following:

- **Reciprocity:** People need to return favors. Doing a favor imposes a debt, and the other person needs to pay it off. If you invite someone to dinner, this person will most likely end up paying you back.

- **Commitment and coherence:** Be and appear coherent with the declarations or with the acts previously carried out. Imagine that you are going to buy a house and the seller indicates the price. You agree and decide to buy it. A few days later, the seller tells you that the price is slightly higher since he had looked at it wrong. As you had already said yes and you had promised, for being consistent, most likely, you will accept the new price.

- **Social approval:** Feeling included. What a large number of people do tends to be considered valid. If all your friends think that a certain brand of car is the most reliable, surely your opinion will end up being the same as theirs. As the saying goes: "too much evil, the consolation of fools."

- **Authority:** The explanations given by someone who considers himself important or who comes from an institution seems more credible. Actor Hugh Laurie has been hired to make drug announcements since, despite not being a doctor, playing one (House series) has given him a similar advertising projection.

- **Sympathy:** When there is physical attraction, it is easier to convince someone of something. Sympathy and similarities are going to be key factors in persuading people. A study from the United States showed that when a woman was charged and went to trial, she received lesser penalties when she was attractive than when she was not.

- **Scarcity:** The perception of scarcity generates demand. When a product is presented as limited in time or accessibility, it leads to a change in purchasing attitude. Many stores use techniques such as offering products or prices for a limited time or offer limited units.

Foot in the door

Within the category of commitment and coherence, we find a famous technique called "the foot in the door." This technique consists of making a small request that the vast majority of people will accept, and then make a larger one, which is the real request.

In 1966 Freedman and Fraser conducted an experiment on the foot in the door. They asked several people to put up a large, ugly sign in their garden that said, "Drive carefully." Only 17% agreed. Another group of people was first asked to sign a document in favor of road safety. This petition involved little commitment, which is why almost everyone signed.

What happened? When, weeks later, they asked this second group to put the poster in their garden, 55% of the people agreed. In this way, you can see how we can be manipulated without realizing it. What we would not do at first, we would access it through a small "manipulative act."

Asch's Experiment

Another classic study in the field of social influence is that of Solomon Asch (1956). This researcher would gather groups of people in one room and show them a line drawing. He then showed them three lines of different sizes, one of which was the same length as the previously shown line and asked them to tell which line was the same length as the first line.

Everyone in the room was in the league, except one. When all the people in agreement agreed that the line of similar size was the wrong one, the participant who did not know anything about what was going on behind their back on several occasions ended up choosing the wrong line as well as the others.

This experiment was carried out with different variants, changing the number of people and the position in which the participant gave his answer. The more people opted for the wrong option before that participant, the more likely they were to choose the majority option. Also, the fact that there was one person who disagreed with the majority made it more likely that the participant chose the correct option and not the one that erroneously indicated the majority.

Milgram's experiment

Finally, another of the classic experiments in psychology is that of Stanley Milgram (1974). This researcher asked a participant to ask questions of another participant who was in a booth. Each time a question failed, the participant had to press a button that administered a shock and raise the voltage.

The participant who answered the questions and received the downloads was an actor who feigned the downloads, which were not real. Most of the participants, despite screaming in pain from the other participant, managed to deliver shocks so strong that they could lead to death. Throughout the process, the researcher told the participant that they should continue.

Subsequently, various studies showed that when people were asked what maximum discharge, they would be able to give, they prevent the authority of the researcher and tend to give low data. However, when they participate in the experiment, the researcher's voice telling them to continue is enough for them to do so.

Forms of social influence

Currently, it is considered that social influence can occur in different ways:

- **Compliance:** Compliance is the degree to which emotions, opinions, or feelings will change to fit the group's opinions. Social groups often have norms and values that indicate what to think and when. If we do not accept it, we will not enter the group. Therefore, to be members of the group we are going to change our opinions for theirs. We are going to settle for what they tell us.

- **Socialization:** Socialization consists of internalizing the norms and ideology of a society. It is a learning process that lasts a lifetime. There are a series of social agents who will transmit the socialization process to us. The most important social agents are the family and the school.

- **Peer pressure:** Peer pressure or social pressure is the influence of a group of peers. This pressure usually occurs from other people like friends and family. The strongest peer pressure may be that of adolescence.

- **Obedience:** Obedience consists of listening to order and following it. Orders can consist of actions that are performed or omitted. In obedience, there is a key figure; that of authority. This can be from a person to a community or an idea. He is a figure who, above all, deserves obedience for different reasons.

- **Leadership:** Leadership is the set of managerial skills to influence the way of being or acting of people or a workgroup. These skills are used to make the person or teamwork enthusiastically achieve their goals and objectives. These capabilities include the ability to delegate, take the initiative, manage, convene, promote, encourage, motivate, and evaluate a project, among others.

- **Persuasion:** Persuasion is a process aimed at changing the attitude or behavior of a person or a group towards some event, idea, object or person. This is done by using words to convey information, feelings, or reasoning, or a combination thereof. It is influencing someone through words. Persuasion is equated with rhetoric.

Cognitive dissonance

But why do all these methods of social influence work? Although there are various explanations, one of the theories that have gained more strength over time is the theory of cognitive dissonance (Festiger, 1957). Cognitive dissonance occurs when two thoughts conflict or when a behavior conflicts by not adapting to previous beliefs (Ex: someone who thinks that killing is bad and ends up killing, someone who thinks that smoking is bad and ends up smoking).

Cognitive dissonance is understood as the tension caused by the lack of internal harmony in the system of ideas, beliefs, and emotions. When two ideas or behaviors with which they are incompatible occur, this tension occurs. The dissonance, and the unpleasant aftertaste it leaves, will lead people to try to restore coherence. Although the reduction of dissonance can occur in different ways, the result is usually a change in attitudes.

An example of how dissonance relates to cognitive dissonance is as follows. Let's say that a person is considered good. Let's imagine that this person participates in the Milgram experiment. Our person considers that it is good to obey authority, and she wants to continue considering herself like this. Therefore, this person will obey the researcher and give stronger shocks each time the other participant fails in the answers. If he did not obey, the dissonance would appear.

She will not consider the option of disobeying because she does not want to distance herself from the attributes that distinguish a good person for her. It is true that she also considers that it is good not to torture others with downloads, but at first, these downloads are slight. So, between the two attributes, at first, she chooses to obey the investigator.

On the other hand, as downloads rise, the power of the two opposing behaviors is also balanced.

In defense of the label that she wants to keep for herself (that of a good person), so that dissonance will also grow.

When this occurs, the person applying the downloads stops managing them or continues. In the first case, to safeguard your image against the fact of having disobeyed, your mind is likely to begin to question that authority. In the second case, for the same purpose, the person can become convinced that the downloads do not cause as much damage as it seems. And the person who receives them is pretending or that they are good for them since, according to the researcher (authority), they improve their learning.

In any case, by opting for one of the two options, your mind will attack the other, so that the person who administers the downloads can continue to consider themselves a good person.

The role of emotions

Until now, we have talked, above all, about changes in attitudes, thoughts, and behaviors, but there is another factor of great importance, emotions. Despite the general idea that emotions follow one path while logical reasoning follows another, this is a fallacy.

According to Damasio (1994), emotions always influence reasoning, even if it is logical. Furthermore, if emotions did not influence, the decisions we would make would not be socially accepted. Think, for example, of psychopaths who do not regulate emotions and fail to empathize. Their decisions are for their benefit, but they leave other people aside.

Therefore, one form of social influence, which is transversal to the other previously explained forms, consists of appealing to emotions. Manipulating emotions is considered, from logic, a fallacy since instead of giving logical reasoning, attempts are made to change emotions so that this results in a change in attitudes. This will especially affect those people who let their emotions greatly influence their reasoning processes.

In conclusion, we could say that it is very easy to influence others, but, in turn, it is no less difficult to be influenced. As we have seen, social groups and people in authority are going to influence us a lot. The best way to manage these influences is to know the mechanisms of influence and try to be aware of when they occur.

CHAPTER 13

THE 4 PERSONALITY TYPES

A group of American researchers suggest that there are four personality types based on five personality traits.

Throughout the history of psychology, various authors have developed different theories of personality, including different personality types. Recently, a group of researchers from the University of the Northwest, in Evanston, Illinois (USA), have carried out an exhaustive analysis of data, the results of which challenge established paradigms in psychology. Martin Gerlach led the study.

Social psychologists question whether personality types exist. Traits are another matter. Personality traits "can be measured consistently across ages, across cultures," said Amaral, co-author of the study, professor of chemical and biological engineering at the McCormick School of Engineering at Northwestern University.

Researchers have reviewed data from more than 1.5 million respondents and found that there are at least four distinct groups of personality types: average, reserved, self-centered, and role model. These four personality types are based on five basic personality traits: neuroticism, extraversion, openness, kindness, and conscience. The new study has been published by the journal Nature Human Behavior.

A still-controversial concept in psychology

William Revelle, professor of psychology at the Weinberg College of Arts and Sciences and lead author of the study, explains that "people have tried to classify personality types since the time of Hippocrates, but previous scientific literature has found that this has not made sense." The data from this new research shows that "there are higher densities of certain personality types."

However, at first, Revelle was skeptical about the premise presented by the study. In psychology, the definition of personality types remains controversial, particularly as empirical support has been given to several classifications. Past attempts focused on small groups of research yielded mostly findings that could not be replicated.

"Forms of personality existed only in the literature of self-help, and had no place in scientific journals," says Amaral. "Because of this analysis, we conclude that this will change now."

Personality types: a new approach

The latest work combined an alternative statistical method with data from four questionnaires of more than

1.5 million respondents from around the world. This consisted of 120 and 300 items collected from John Johnson's IPIP-NEO, respectively, the "myPersonality" project and the data sets from the evidence of the BBC's great personality.

The questionnaires, developed by the research community for decades, have between 44 and 300 questions. People voluntarily respond to online questionnaires, attracted by the opportunity to receive comments about their personality.

From this large set of data, the team of researchers identified the five traits that are perhaps most widely accepted: neuroticism, extraversion, openness, kindness, and awareness. After developing new algorithms, four personality groups or types emerged:

- **Average rate.** Normal people are high in neuroticism and extraversion and low in transparency. According to the researchers, women are more likely to belong to the average type.

- **Reserved type.** The reserved type is emotionally stable, as well as not very neurotic. Those who belong to this group are not particularly extraverted, which does not mean that their treatment is pleasant.

- **Model to follow.** People belonging to the Role Model personality type have a low score in neuroticism and a high score in all other traits. The probability that someone is a role model increases dramatically with age. According to the researchers, these are trustworthy people and open to new ideas, and they are good people to be in charge of things. They also say that women are more likely to belong to this group.

- **Self-centered people.** Self-centered people score high in extraversion and are below average in openness, kindness, and conscience. There is a very drastic decline in the number of egocentric forms in both females and males as people age.

Personality changes throughout life

The researchers explain that as people mature, their personality settings change. For example, older people tend to be less neurotic, though more aware and personable than people under the age of 20.

"When we look at large population groups, it is clear that there are trends, and that these trends can also change over time, " Amaral said.

CHAPTER 14

THE SECRETS OF SUBLIMINAL PSYCHOLOGY

The subliminal is that which is below the threshold of consciousness. When the term is applied to a stimulus, it refers to the fact that it is not perceived consciously, but it still influences behavior.

A subliminal message is designed for the recipient to receive on an unconscious level. It may be, for example, an image that is transmitted so briefly that consciousness does not notice it, but it is etched in memory.

It is said that subliminal content is used by some advertising, although the transmission of such messages usually in advertising is punishable by law. With subliminal advertising, it is possible to present a product or service to the consumer so that the consumer feels like acquiring it without knowing the authentic reasons that lead to this.

For example, there are those who say that the Coca-Cola bottle has the shape of a woman's silhouette, to subliminally "conquer" those who feel sexual attraction to the female gender.

It should be remembered that subliminal publicity is not associated with advertisements in connection with social groups, a practice that is legally legitimate, and does nothing unconscious. An example of associative advertising is tobacco commercials, which often show smokers as sensual and interesting subjects, happy and proud of their lives. They show no trace of the fundamental reasons that lead a person to smoke: stress, personal dissatisfaction, shyness, and insecurity, among others. In this way, the consumer can interpret that if he smokes, he will obtain, for example, success on the sentimental level.

Subliminal positive affirmations

Finally, we can mention positive subliminal affirmations, which are phrases that are recorded so that the receiver listens to them repeatedly, and their unconscious assimilates the information. Positive subliminal affirmations are used to quit smoking or eliminate phobias, for example.

Subliminal tools in entertainment

Derren Brown is a very famous British mentalist and illusionist in his land, who, in recent years, has made all kinds of shows on theater and television to try to convince his viewers of the truth of his power. Their tricks usually have a common denominator: making the participant discover a secret on their own, without even knowing how they did it.

In 2009, a special that he made on English television was very popular, through which he tried to generate a kind of collective hypnosis, making his viewers believe that they were going to connect in a large energy network ... or lie. During the minutes before the moment long-awaited by millions of English people tired of the crude and boring reality, Derren explained that it would be necessary to sit in a comfortable position. They would need to be watching the television closely for a few seconds, after which, he assured, the entire public he would share the feeling of not being able to get up from the seat no matter how hard he tried.

He also warned that one could suffer from profound exhaustion and even dizziness so that those who were not willing to provoke this state chose to stay out of the experiment. Fortunately for the unbelievers, but unfortunately for the billionaire man of the show, the broadcast of the program on the Internet exposed the trick that did affect viewers: a series of unpleasant and grim images were broadcast for very short periods throughout the alleged hypnosis, without being seen on a conscious level.

Subliminal Persuasion

Subliminal programming has always had some enigmatic pictures in it. While it has become more popular lately, it is still kept by many people at an arm's length. Perhaps they are not completely ready to believe in its efficacy, or they are rather apprehensive about using it, and what they might do with their lives.

But subliminal persuasion is not some hidden hocus pocus, although it is very successful and strong. It all revolves around the subconscious mind's energy. In using subliminal manipulation, you are making full use of your mind's unbounded capabilities. And this ability is the product of our mind's inherent strength. There is nothing wrong with using it to make our lives easier. It is only natural for us to learn how it functions and use it to live life to its full potential.

And once you have opened yourself to this influence, you can take advantage of subliminal persuasion. It will help to make the conditions more favorable. Below are The Secrets of Subliminal Psychology to achieving meaningful results in daily circumstances.

1. **Psychology in reverse.**

    Reverse psychology is one of the subliminal persuasion techniques, which is the easiest and most effective. Unfortunately, it is being used by a lot of people now, and it has become quite a popular term. People have started using it too overtly, and that has weakened its usefulness because many people know reverse psychology automatically when they see it. Yet that does not mean that when you have any persuading to do, you should take it out.

Reverse psychology makes use of the power of subliminal persuasion, and you can always rely on its persuasive ability. And the trick is to use it subtly. If you use the same scripts on reverse psychology, tell them in a way that hides the fact that you are using a strategy of persuasion. Nevertheless, it can produce unexpected results when used correctly.

2. Bring coincidences together.

A coincidence is another important instrument that can be used for subliminal persuasion. Most people no longer necessarily believe in coincidences, but others still do. Then there are also a lot of people who think that they are not believers but are often persuaded when they find a very shocking one. It can still be very convincing to see correlations between things and find sense in them.

And if you want to convince anyone to do so, you could use coincidences. The problem is, how is that possible? You can't make coincidences happen after all; otherwise, they'll no longer be coincidences. Okay, by designing and organizing situations and events, you can make coincidences appear to happen, but subtly, so as not to show that they are occurring by design.

3. Enlist senses of the people.

Speech can be a straightforward weapon of persuasion, but if you want to persevere a little more subtly, why don't you target the other senses? Place an idea in someone's mind, for example, use a perfume that will remind the person of something relevant to what you want.

4. Calling a person by his first name.

Did you know that the simple act of calling someone by the first name is already a powerful technique of subliminal persuasion? There is no conclusive justification as to why this works, but it does. Others claim to do so helps make requests more intimate, so he or she feels more committed and becomes more likely to act on them.

Subliminal Psychology in An Intimate Relationship

Relationships require a lot of time; the work involved in sustaining a relationship will, in reality, never end. Unfortunately, there are a lot of factors outside our control that relationships often seem to take a backseat in life. This, and because these relationships are by nature highly reactive, they are easily weakened over time. But some of the strongest marriages buckle down under life's stresses and demands.

It is natural to go through rough patches in a relationship. But if issues aren't immediately fixed, they begin to pile up and accumulate. There comes a make or break point in most relationships. When you're on the verge of a broken relationship, turning it around isn't too late.

1. Un-Pollute the Mind and Connection.

It can still save all troubled relationships. The reason a lot of people settle for going their separate ways is that they don't know how to solve the issues that arise in the relationship correctly.

But the fact is, the reasons you first joined the relationship are still there. Most likely, they just got lost under all the stresses, expectations, environmental factors, negative talk and understanding of relationships in general, and so forth. Add to that all the unresolved problems that trigger negative emotions like mistrust, fear, doubt, and suppressed anger.

All you have to do to save a relationship is to unravel the reasons and strengthen them again. Remember why you were interested in the relationship and see if those reasons still hold. If they do, it's all just a matter of removing all the relationship-damaging layers accumulated that pollute the relationship.

How will you take these off?

2. **Attract Positive Improvements as Substitution.**

Now that all those undermining layers are gone, you have plenty of room in your relationship for positive changes. Imagining the kind of relationship you want to have invites an instant positive change in your relationship. Focus your mind on the positive changes in the relationship you want to see happen. Invite these thoughts and improvements by the use of strong subliminal messages into actualization.

Subliminal messages have the power to control your conduct and acts. And if you fill your mind with them, you'll certainly see changes happening.

And what changes will subliminal messages and couple self-help welcome into your revived relationship?

- Help you overcome frustrating feelings

- Allow you to step forward and leave your old baggage behind

- Help you settle disagreements and come up with mutually beneficial solutions

- Help you see and embrace personality differences

- Shape a common vision

- Deepen confidence

- Make a relationship

It will not be sufficient to save a relationship cycle without plans for future problems that are sure to come. And if after a while you don't want to end up in the same make or break point again, you've got to learn how to manage the relationship properly.

It does not take an expert to fix issues with the partnership. You don't need to go straight to ask a counselor. There are plenty of tips on self-help relationships, and you can work out things together and as one.

CHAPTER 15

HOW TO USE DARK PSYCHOLOGY IN SEDUCTION

The reason seduction is a mind game is that most people have deep psychological needs that are not satisfied. You can seduce your target if you find out the needs of the other person and put yourself in such a way that you can suggest that you can satisfy them. The explanation behind this is that we're driven more than anything by our feelings, given what we'd like to believe. If there is a conflict between reason and heart inside our-selves, the heart always wins. Read on and learn how to use these timeless seduction rules.

You must stand for something, and you must embody something. You can tailor that to your target e.g., if they like the quiet, sensitive, saintly but secretly sexually threatening type, you can become that. Be mysterious. Always, even after a relationship begins, maintain the mystery, keep some corners dark. Display a blank, mysterious face onto which people can project their fantasies. People are dying to be allowed to fantasize about you—do not spoil this golden opportunity by overexposing yourself. Familiarity is the death of seduction. Never declare your feelings for your target. Never say, 'I love you.' Instead, mention your feelings. Love not stated speaks volumes. Be ambiguous, hard to figure out.

Low self-esteem is repellent. Don't put yourself down and don't show weakness. People treat you as you treat yourself, and if they sense weakness, they pounce on it. What is natural to your character is inherently seductive. Appearing to be secure is sexy. However, displaying overt strength and power is not. Learn to play up your natural weaknesses and flaws after the person has known you for a while. Having an air of sadness is seductive, especially if that sadness appears to be spiritual in origin and not merely a product of a depressed mood. Depth and complexity draw people in. Anything that cannot be understood is seductive. Always be positive. Take a step back, be distant, narcissistic. Never appear jealous but make people jealous by hinting that you may not be that interested in them.

To appear charismatic, keep the source of your charisma secret. Charisma springs from and plays on repressed sexuality. Because their lack of freedom oppresses most people, they are drawn by people who appear to be more free and fluid. Dandies are subtle and never try hard to gain attention—small touches produce the effect they create. At all costs, you must embody something, anything to avoid the taint of familiarity and commonness. Do not allow yourself to be easily manipulated—you appear less attractive that way—attractive traits: being a leader, knowledgeable in many subjects, good conversationalist, not appearing needy. Appear to be desireless. Appear to be excellent. Do not flirt blatantly—send mixed signals

CHAPTER 16

GAMES THEORY

Have you noticed that an opponent has a particular mania, for example, that he tends to joke when he has an excellent hand but that he remains silent when he bluffs? This is very good, psychology is a formidable weapon in poker, and this observation could be useful for you, provided you know how to use it.

When you have noticed, thanks to an opponent's tell, a defect in his game, you must be patient. In poker, the strokes follow each other but are not alike, and you may need to play a hundred hands with this opponent before the situation happens again. Even if it does happen again, you have to be in a position to win the pot.

If you recognize a tell from a player that he is bluffing, but you do not have enough play to beat a bluff, do not pay even if you know full well that your opponent is cheekily lying. The goal of poker is not to be right but to make money!

... And use it with discretion.

It is very important to be discreet when using an opponent's tell. On the one hand, so that he does not notice it, and on the other hand, so that the other players of the table do not notice it. Not see either, so there is no point in claiming on all the rooftops that you paid a bluff because your opponent's right hand was shaking, even if they are accusing you of having played badly.

The most important thing in poker is to get the most out of the shots and keep your weapons and their secret benefits as long as possible. The more people around the table were trying to exploit a tell, the less it will earn you money.

Professional players know how to handle tells and push psychology even further, they can lead you to believe that they make mistakes only to surprise you when you think you can exploit them. Beware of tells that are too big to be true.

Tells like deception

As you can guess above, even if you are not good at psychology or observation and you do not spot the tells of your opponents, you can still use this facet of poker. Lots of professional players only play with pot odds and the value of their hands, without the tells, especially when they come from the internet world, so you don't have to worry.

Manipulate your opponents by making them believe you have a major mistake, and we can see this action to a lesser degree in online poker with players who "tank" (think for a long time) before jumping into it all in. Whether they played the watch (or, on the contrary, they behaved almost instantly) remains to be seen to make you think they're bluffing or, because they've got an excellent deck.

CONCLUSION

It is time to conclude from these findings that social norms, rules, and values are "not natural" for human beings, and that society frequently imposes group action based on what the powerful want over the powerless. Because survival mentality is our norm, what society is attempting to do is to regulate the wild beast in every human being. This is done by educating them from an early age to follow the control group's laws, rules, and morality, typically the wealthy, who dominate our governments and institutions. Therefore, should we denounce those who feel that society does not give them a reasonable deal-who will, in turn, take what they need to survive in an often hostile world where privilege depends on your education, family, or wealth? Will psychology itself have to come out of the closet and accept that normal human conduct is in contrast to strict structures and regulations? That people hate society, but they experience some helplessness in trying to survive among the sheep because they are powerless against those who regulate the law-making and morality? Is it any wonder that sometimes an alone person takes it into their own hands to change society or their own life to live a freer self-controlled existence away from the rigors of societies? Which all inevitably crumble and reinvent themselves as the newly rich and the powerful take control once again? Over the last century, we saw China turning itself from an empire dominated by depots into a military dictatorship controlled by the rich and powerful into a communist look of the 1950s in which Communism will decide a decent life for all.

The China of today as a capitalist democratic state is based on a political party that decides the lives of the poor people, who fought for it. Will there be another revolution in China in the future? It seems doubtful at the moment, given the turmoil in many parts of China by minorities unable to comply with the central rule. Could not all powers see their downfall! Can psychology then answer this problem of human actions as a basic survival mechanism because, in reality, human beings are inherently aggressive, cruel, and superior over those who are weaker than themselves? In mental institutions, psychiatry is also seen as the agents of social order—if you disagree with society and its laws. Then you must be insane—thus you should be arrested and regulated for the health and good of all.

On the other hand, psychology is seen as the therapeutic component of mental wellbeing, where we help those who are out of step with culture find their position and fit back into what is considered common behavior for that group. What is the answer to those who revolt against the society in which they live and want a better way of life out of the control of the powerful and the right to live a life they want as their own? And are we waiting for the films to come true? The tragedy that threatens all humans and a return to the life of a dog eat dog called survival—the real social norm!